GW01018322

Contents

Helion & Company Limited
Unit 8 Amherst Business Centre
Budbrooke Road
Warwick
CV34 5WE
England
Tel. 01926 499 619
Email: info@helion.co.uk
Website: www.helion.co.uk
Twitter: @helionbooks
Visit our blog http://blog.helion.co.uk/

Text © Javier García de Gabiola 2021
Colour profiles © Tom Cooper and Anderson
      Subtil 2021
Maps © Tom Cooper and Anderson Subtil
      2021
Photographs © as individually credited

Designed & typeset by Farr out Publications,
      Wokingham, Berkshire
Cover design by Paul Hewitt, Battlefield
      Design (www.battlefield-design.co.uk)

ISBN 978-1-914377-01-3

British Library Cataloguing-in-Publication
      Data
A catalogue record for this book is available
      from the British Library

We always welcome receiving book
proposals from prospective authors.

Note: In order to simplify the use of this book, all names, locations and geographic
designations are as provided in *The Times World Atlas*, or other traditionally accepted
major sources of reference, as of the time of described events.

Acknowledgements

I would like to dedicate this work to my wife, Carolina Martínez Zamora, for her support and patience while finishing this book during the holidays in Puerto de Mazarrón, Murcia, in August 2021, and to my fathers-in-law, Chitina Martínez Zamora (as she kindly left us in her nice house on the beach), and Juan de la Cruz Martínez Manuel, whose father fought as a captain and was severely wounded in the Larache sector during the Rif War.

Introduction

The Rif War in rugged Northern Morocco is remembered for the romantic novels and films about the French Foreign Legion, such as Gary Cooper's *Beau Geste*. In reality, the French intervention, although very important, was later (only in 1925–1926) and secondary in importance to that of the Spanish. Spain had been fighting in Africa since 1909, suffering disasters such as Barranco del Lobo and experiencing victories such as the cavalry charge at Taxdirt. Madrid had to face enemies such as El Mizzián, El Jeriro, or the famous El Raisuni, who was played by Sean Connery in *The Wind and the Lion*. Later, Abd el-Krim's revolt caused 8,000 Spanish deaths at Annual in 1921, and then loomed over French Morocco, leading to another 5,700 casualties. This war was not only a campaign of attacks by Rif guerrillas on isolated forts and columns, but degenerated into trench warfare in some sectors, and saw the use of tanks, artillery, gas, aviation, and an amphibious operation that would go on to be closely studied by the Allies in the Second World War. All of this forced an effective collaboration between Generals Philippe Petain and Miguel Primo de Rivera who, as allies, finally crushed the rebellion after gathering some 250,000 soldiers and 300 aircraft against some 30–40,000 Rifians.

The young Francisco Franco as a cadet at the age of 14 in 1907, who would become the most famous military man of the Rif War, becoming a general at the end of it and then dictator of Spain after the civil war of 1936. (via Gárate Córdoba)

This work will deal with the organisation of the Spanish and Rifian armies but also of the air forces and their operations, including those of an incipient and frustrated Rifian aviation. Also, in the case of Spain, the Rif War was the birth certificate of its air forces in combat and here, Spain was the first nation to use specially designed bomb-aiming devices. The war also saw the Spanish army completely reformed, reaching new levels of effectiveness with the founding of the Spanish Legion and the recruitment of Moroccan soldiers of the *Regulares*. These troops, together with a plethora of commanders who made their combat debuts here, such as Franco, Mola, Queipo de Llano, Varela, Yagüe and Kindelán amongst others, would later fight in the Spanish Civil War. These commanders would be called the "Africanistas" (Africanists) and would constitute the hard core of the military that rose up against the government in 1936.

Finally, before going into this history, it is recommend that the reader take a close look at the map of the Spanish Protectorate in Morocco in the colour section of this book, and to refer to it while reading this work. Also, several black and white maps are included in this work for the reader's reference at the appropriate time. I ask for the reader's patience and indulgence, since the military operations in this war were extremely convoluted, with names of cities, rivers, mountains, characters and geographical features extremely unfamiliar to the Western reader, not to mention the language in which they are designated, in Arabic. On the other hand, Spanish is not a language very well known to the Anglo-Saxon reader, nor is it very widespread outside the Peninsula and

Francisco Franco at the age of 16 as 2nd Lieutenant of Infantry assigned to the Zamora Regiment, in El Ferrol, Galicia, in 1909, at the beginning of the Rif War. (via Gárate Córdoba)

Latin America. I hope I have made all this gibberish a little more intelligible, even if it is by abusing indications such as "further north", "further south", etcetera. In any case, a useful way to follow these operations, at least in a general way, is to trace the movements following the geographical division of Morocco into kabyles. For this reason, I have also allowed myself to note in brackets almost constantly the location of each village or geographical feature in one of these kabyles, even at the risk of being reiterative. This will make the reading much more productive, even if it is to the detriment of the literary style.

Spain in Africa

1898 was the year of disaster for Spain. Madrid lost the last remnants of its four centuries of overseas empire: Cuba, Puerto Rico, the Philippines and the Pacific islands. Its possessions passed to a new, young and thriving empire that had just emerged: the United States. Somehow, to compensate for the humiliation and in a context in which all the European powers were dividing up Africa, Spain saw an opportunity to redeem its damaged reputation. However, Spain's relations with North Africa were even older than those with America and as far back as Roman times the Diocese of Hispania included Tingitania Mauritania, nowadays Northern Morocco. In 711, the Arab invasion came from present-day Morocco, and at the end of the Christian Reconquest, in 1497, Spain once again set foot in Africa when the Duke of Medina Sidonia took Melilla by surprise. Cardinal Cisneros, the brilliant regent of Castile after the death of Queen Isabella, continued the conquest of strongpoints on the African coast to control Barbary piracy in the Western Mediterranean, such as Mazalquivir (Mers-el-Quivir, Algeria) in 1505, the Rock of Velez (1508), and culminating with the conquest of Oran (1509), Bejaia, the Rock of Algiers and even Tripoli, in Libya, in 1510. Most of these possessions in Algeria and Libya were lost during the sixteenth century, along with others won and lost such as Bona, Bizerte, Tunis and the Goleta. Others, such as Oran were lost in 1708 but recovered and remained in Spanish hands until 1791. In Morocco, Tangier (Tánger) and Larache were lost in the seventeenth century. On the other hand, Melilla, and Ceuta (the latter since 1580, with the conquest of Portugal), have remained in Spanish hands ever since and, therefore, before the very existence of a Kingdom of Morocco. The area was fragmented into several

principalities that would not begin the road to unity until decades later with the coming of the Alaouite dynasty, the current reigning house, in 1666. Even so, today Morocco continues to claim Ceuta, Melilla, the Rock of Al Hoceima (Alhucemas, in Spanish) and the Rock of Velez as part of its territory.[1]

In 1830 the Spanish presence in North Africa was replaced by that of the French, who began their intervention in Algeria and Morocco. Spain reacted, and in 1838 overtook a French fleet by only a few days before reaching the shore, and occupied the islets of Chafarinas, between the coast of Morocco and Algeria, which virtually began to mark the eastern limit of Spanish influence. In 1857, a series of clashes between the Moors and the outer defensive posts of the garrison of Ceuta, which the kabyle Anyera demanded be abolished, led to the First Moroccan War. The acceptance of Spanish conditions by the new Sultan of Morocco Muley Mohammed came too late, and General Leopoldo O'Donnell invaded Morocco from Ceuta in 1859, reaching Tetuán (Tetouan) and then Tánger (Tangier). Spain won the famous battles of Castillejos, Tetouan and Wad Ras. The peace was signed on 26 April 1860, but it was said that, with 10,000 Spanish casualties, it was a big war, but a small peace: simply a compensation for war expenses, to extend the perimeter of Ceuta and Melilla, and some rights of occupation in Ifni, opposite the Canary Islands, which would not be exercised until 1934. The Most Favoured Nation trade treaty was soon extended to France and the United Kingdom, so that the economic advantages of the war came to nothing vis-à-vis the most aggressive European powers. For Morocco, however, it was an unmitigated disaster, as it gradually opened the country to foreign occupation and the loss of its sovereignty. In 1893 war broke out again, this time to maintain and slightly extend the perimeter of Melilla, again being won by Spain. The Sultan agreed with Spain to punish the kabyles who were harassing Melilla and to create a neutral zone.[2]

The Decomposition of Morocco

In 1898, apart from the Cuba and Philippines disasters, the famous Fashoda Incident happened: the British Empire deprived France of access to East Africa and so Paris sought compensation in the Maghreb and began the dismemberment of the Jerifian

The City of Melilla, first conquered by Spain in 1497, before the existence of a Kingdom of Morocco. In the background Mount Gourougou can be seen, scene of battles in 1909 and 1921. (via Gárate Córdoba)

The Khalifa Muley el Mehdi, saluted by General José Marina, was a Prince of the Moroccan royal house, who ruled the north of Morocco with a certain independence, but was considered by some as a puppet of the Spaniards. General Marina was the military governor of Melilla and commander of the Spanish forces in the 1909–1912 wars. (Biblioteca Nacional via Villalobos)

The Zoco (market) of Marrakech, at the beginning of the twentieth century. The city was the home of Muley Hafid, who rebelled against his brother, becoming the new Sultan of Morocco but was unable to control further rebellions. (Biblioteca Nacional via Villalobos)

(Xerifian) Empire or Kingdom of Morocco. The reason was the instability within it: the Jerife (Xerife), considered a descendant of the Prophet Mohammed, was accepted as Sultan or Prince of the Believers by the various Moroccan regions with the support of the Majzén (Makhzen), or caste of palace bureaucrats who ran the government. But in practice there were some areas that only recognised this authority in theory, and ruled independently, such as the Rif area, or with a great deal of autonomy by royal princes or Jalifas (Khalifas), such as the ones of Fez or Marrakech. In addition, there were seven ports in the empire, governed by the Bajás, or governors, in Tangier, Larache, Rabat, Casablanca, Magazán, Mogador and Safi, which due to their commercial relations with Europe also had some autonomy and even diplomatic functions. Thus, there was a government (or Makhzen country), in the coastal plain and the main cities, and a rebel one (or es-Siba country), in the mountainous interior, such as the Rif, the Yebala (Jebala) or the Atlas.[3]

The Sultan of Morocco from 1912, Muley Yusef, direct ancestor of the kings Mohammed V, Hassan II, and Mohammed VI. (Maurice Bronger/ Roger Viollet, via Courcelle et Marmié)

After the defeat of 1893, the new Sultan Abd el-Aziz had to face a widespread rebellion. In the region of Taza, south-west of Melilla but now inside French Morocco, El Roghi Bu Hamara, who pretended to be the Sultan's brother, rose up in 1902. At the same time, in the region of Tangier, El Raisuni was operating with a troop of bandits, and in Marrakech the Sultan's brother, Muley Hafid, had rebelled. Meanwhile, Spain and France were already agreeing on their spheres of influence: the French proposal for the division of the territory of 1902, which was very generous and left three of the five million Moroccans under Spanish rule, together with Fez and Taza, and was negotiated by the liberals under President Sagasta, was not signed by the conservative Silvela so as not to annoy London. Thus, the new demarcation of 1904 was much poorer for Spain, losing these last two cities and leaving it only the coast and poor strip of land north of the river Lucus. In 1908, the Sultan abdicated to his rebel brother Muley Hafid, but his nationalist reaction was not enough to avoid the consequences of the Algeciras Act of 1906. According to this treaty, the United Kingdom renounced Morocco in exchange for Tangier being declared a neutral zone, and Spain and France assumed police functions to preserve the rights of their citizens and their commercial interests according to the previously agreed lines of influence. Thus, with the excuse of unrest, France occupied Oujda (Uxda) in 1907, bombarded and took Casablanca, and penetrated through the Chaouia region. In 1911, Muley Hafid had to ask France for help to stay in power, and the French army entered Fez, the Moroccan capital. In 1912, the Sultan abdicated to another brother, Muley Yusef, and the French and Spanish governments signed the agreement establishing the Protectorate. But Spain had already been at war in Morocco for several years, since 1909.[4]

Spain, and the "Guy of the Female Donkey"

El Roghi's career was one of the most astonishing in Africa at this time. An official of the Makhzen, he was imprisoned for forging an imperial seal on a document. Pardoned, he emigrated to Algeria, where he contacted the French government and the adventurer Gabriel Debrel, probably becoming an agent of Paris. In 1902 he returned to Taza, Morocco, on the back of a female donkey, for which he was called Bu Hamara, "the guy of the female donkey". In the words of Villalobos, he had 'the virtue of a holy man, the thaumaturgic skills of a magician and the loquacity

El Roghi, "the Guy with the Female Donkey", was probably a French agent, and defeated the Xerifian forces, becoming semi-independent in the Eastern Rif until expelled by the Beni Urriaguels in 1908. (via Marín Ferrer)

The Xerifian (Jerifian, in Spanish) Army, seen here on parade, would fight the rebels in the Rif or other regions of Morocco. It did it with so little success that it attracted the "help" of the Spanish and French forces. (García Figueras, Biblioteca Nacional via Villalobos)

Another view of El Roghi, shown not on a donkey but on a horse. (via Carrasco y De Mesa)

of a charlatan'. He pretended to be the brother of the Sultan, who was in prison, and as the latter was one-eyed, El Roghi spoke to his followers with a squinted eye. In a short time, he took control of Taza, and even threatened Fez, but then moved his base in 1903 to Zeluán (Selouane), in the future Spanish zone of influence, 30km south of Melilla. There, he virtually took control of the whole of Guelaya by 1908, defeating all the Sultan's expeditions, but collecting taxes in his name. As effective ruler of the area, Spain and General Marina made direct agreements with him for the occupation of La Restinga (on the Quebdana coast, south-east of Melilla), and Cabo de Agua (on the Algerian border), as well as granting rights over the mines of Beni Bu Ifrur. However, ambition blinded El Roghi who tried to collect taxes in the central Rif, in Beni Urriaguel. This kabyle, the most numerous and fierce of the whole region, rejected his forces and produced an uprising of the whole of Guelaya against him when he was retreating. Beni Sicar, Beni Sidel, Beni Bu Gafar and Mazuza revolted, expelling El Roghi from Selouane on 5 December. The power vacuum was not filled by the Beni Urriaguel but by Mohammed Amezian or El Mizzián, the leader of Beni Bu Ifrur, where the mines coveted by the Spanish were located. So, El Mizzián became Spain's enemy for the next five years. On 5 July 1909, El Mizzián, after waiting for the return of the Rifians who were seasonal workers in Algeria, met with El Chadly, Mazuza's kaid (the chief of the tribe or kabyle), and agreed to the expulsion of the Spanish miners from Beni Bu Ifrur. The Rif War, the War of Africa or Second Moroccan War, as it was called in Spain, had begun. Nobody could foresee that it would cause the fall of governments, the coming of a dictatorship, and that the war would last until 1927.[5]

1

The Spanish and Rifian Armies

In 1909 the Spanish Army was made up of conscripts with little motivation due to its non-voluntary nature. The very basic training of the soldiers made it necessary to control them by marching in close order, precisely the least ideal way for fighting in the broken terrain of the Rif. Along with the 70 (later 78) line

regiments, each consisting of three battalions (*Batallón de Infantería de Línea*) totalling 3,000 men, Spain created the so-called *Cazadores* battalions (*Batallón de Cazadores* – light infantry battalion, literally "Hunters Battalion") to better adapt to the African terrain. The Cazadores were in theory select shock troops and agile when

King Alfonso XIII of Spain visited the Rif in 1911 and promoted a policy of intervention in Morocco, hence being called "The African". He supported the dictatorship of General Primo de Rivera in September of 1923 as a way to avoid the scandal of the publication of the Picasso File about the Disaster of Annual, and also to finish the Rif War. Despite monarchist parties winning a narrow majority in the 1931 elections, he elected to leave Spain when the republicans won most of the cities. (via Marín Ferrer)

manoeuvring, but their soldiers were the same conscripts as in the line regiments. However, they had some above-average quality, and they were systematically sent to Africa to lead offensives, until the appearance of the Moroccan indigenous regular troops in 1912, and later the *Tercio de la Legión* in 1920. On the other hand, the bulk of the troops annihilated at Annual were line troops and not Cazadores, and in the subsequent victorious campaigns between 1925 and 1927, the Cazadores continued to serve as battle forces, although they generally occupied the positions newly conquered by the shock troops, while the line were relegated to fixed garrison

duty at the hundreds of defensive posts. Therefore, some qualified training for mountain warfare must have been given to the Cazadores. In 1909 there were 23 battalions, each consisting of four companies (and one depot) at 302 men per company, 1,206 per battalion, full strength. The Cazadores were grouped in Half Brigades with three other battalions from the same province, and together with those from neighbouring provinces formed brigades of six battalions, reinforced with machine gun sections. The five battalions of the Balearic and Canary Islands, on the other hand, were independent. With the line troops, although initially whole regiments served in Africa (but with their battalions serving separately in different sectors), later, Expeditionary Battalions were formed from the Peninsular line regiments, or their 1st Battalion was sent to Africa, with a number of loose companies selected from a regiment and sent to Africa to form a battalion.[1]

The equipment of both Cazadores and line troops was the white striped uniform, the famous "Rayadillo", which was fresh and very comfortable, and similar to the famous uniform worn during the war in Cuba, although the separation between the blue lines was 1cm greater, giving the appearance of being totally white. Footwear in the field of Valencian espadrilles with black ribbons, though rustic, was however ideal for the long marches and the heat and dryness of the African terrain. On their heads they wore the typical Spanish *Ros*, similar to the French *kepi*, lined in white and with a duchesse cover to protect their necks from the sun. Progressively the *Ros* was replaced by British Wolseley salacots (sun helmets) bought in Gibraltar. The Cazadores' belt was the black leather Model 1895, modified for Mauser ammunition, with two front cartridge pouches and a larger rear one with capacity for three ammunition packs, and a machete buckle. The backpack was made of strong white canvas with a green bugle on its flap. They also had a tin cup, regulation since 1893, which was placed on the front belt buckle, and a wineskin as a canteen. Their equipment was completed with a dark brown blanket. On 20 June 1914 the Spanish uniform changed to the dark greenish khaki, which in practice became more of a light brown.

The troops were armed with the Spanish Mauser rifle Model 1893 of 7mm calibre and holding five cartridges (later replaced by Mauser 1916), and usually the Model 1879 machete. As for the machine guns, the initial meagre 12 Maxim Nordenfelts existing since 1907, assigned only to the 2nd Cazadores Brigade, were supplemented with 20 Hotchkiss guns in 1908. In September 1909, the Brigades of the Reinforced Division and the 3rd Cazadores Brigade still had only 24 machine guns, and the 1st Brigade only four, at the rate of two machine guns per section. In 1910 there were 48 guns, but the 12 Maxims were relegated to fixed positions. In 1914 another 20 Hotchkiss guns were purchased, forming machine gun companies made up of four guns (two sections), one for each line or Cazadores

Cazadores in a trench, wearing the "Rayadillo" uniform with the blue and red barrack cap, instead of the Wolseley salacot or the Ros cap. (via Fernández Riera)

battalion. With the First World War in progress, Spain could not buy new guns, having to manufacture the new Hotchkiss models in Oviedo. By 1920, the complement was increased to eight machine guns per company. Finally, the Colt machine gun Model 1915 was supplied to the cavalry in 1916. As will be seen in the exposition of the Spanish tactics employed, the higher proportion of machine guns in the Regulares and Legion units was an important factor in the success of the latter units.[2]

The prevailing tactics employed a line of riflemen consisting of one or two rifle companies, with a depth of two to three soldiers. The vanguard was supported by troops of the same company who were in the rear to reinforce it in case it was necessary to make the assault. These were close, but at the same time, out of reach of enemy fire. Behind this front line were the reinforcement troops at battalion level, and two other companies. In total the battalion had between four and six companies, and later a company of Colt or Hotchkiss machine guns was

Policía Indígena showing off their shooting skills, while standing on their mounts and wearing campaign dress. (via Gárate Córdoba)

Tangiers *Policía Indígena* in barracks dress during training. (via Carrasco and de Mesa)

added. Although in theory the formation was that of skirmishing, as mentioned before, to control the recruits who were not yet qualified individual fighters, the real formation was that of close order, the battalion occupying a space of 400 to 500 metres of front by 300 to 600 metres in depth. For this reason, the troops, being concentrated, were subjected to Rifian fire until at short range, at which point a bayonet assault would be used to occupy the position, because the Moors were afraid of the physical clash, much like the Boers or the Americans against the British. The inexperience of the recruits forced the officers and chiefs to expose themselves to much enemy fire to direct the recruits and to set an example and boost morale, but when a number of them fell in combat, the troops, terrified and uncontrolled, panicked, as happened in the Barranco del Lobo.[3]

The Native Troops Arrive

From the first experiences with the recruits, the conclusion was reached that it was useful to have better trained soldiers and good individual marksmen, who were more aggressive and knew the terrain and the Rifian customs and how to use them to their advantage. To do this, there was nothing better than to start recruiting Moroccan soldiers into the service of Spain, many of them former Rifian guerrillas who fought as such. These soldiers were volunteers and received a salary and it was

a first step to creating professional armed forces. The first unit, although surplus for the time being, was the Indigenous Police (*Policía Indígena*) formed in the recently occupied Cabo de Agua and La Restinga in 1908, which in December 1909 expanded to three companies on foot and another on horseback with kabyle men from Guelaya. In January 1912 there were already 663 men grouped in six *Mías* (companies), one per tribe or kabyle (cabila, in Spanish): the 1st Quebdana, 2nd Mazuza, 3rd Beni Sicar, 4th Beni Bu Ifrur, 5th Beni Bu Gafar and 6th Beni Sidel. Between 1910 and 1912, *Tabors* (or light battalions) were also created in the western zone of the Protectorate, named after Tangier, Tetouan, Larache and Casablanca (later called Tetouan), Larache, Alcazarquivir and Arcila, with three Mías each, at the rate of 254 soldiers in each Tabor. In 1920 there were already 30 Mías in the whole Protectorate. However, with the disaster of Annual in 1921 practically all the Indigenous Police deserted or were annihilated. Their forces were replaced by the so-called Yaich of Abd el-Kader, in Beni Sicar, which would guard Guelaya. From 1922 they progressively became part of the Mehalas, another native unit, as shown below.[4]

More reliable and with better results were the so-called *Regulares*, created by Lieutenant Colonel Dámaso Berenguer Fusté. These were also composed of Moroccan volunteers with Spanish commanders. Being a shock unit, the most aggressive and

Tangiers *Policía Indígena* in barracks dress learning the Spanish language. (via Carrasco and de Mesa)

and more flexible units. The 2nd Group was annihilated or deserted en masse during the Disaster of Annual in 1921, but Spain still kept its confidence in these units. However, sometimes they were only issued with enough rifles for the sentries and the rifles were chained in place, and there were cases in which they were given "a pile of stones for all their armament". In 1922 the 5th Alhucemas Group was created, and in 1924 a fourth Tabor was added to each of the Groups, which were all infantry from 1921, although they later became three infantry and one cavalry, except for Larache, which had

competent officers asked to be assigned there, so that the quality of the unit improved substantially, becoming an elite corps. Thus, Franco himself, José Sanjurjo, Emilio Mola, José Millán-Astray, Juan Yagüe and José Enrique Varela, future rebel leaders during the civil war, were trained and served in the Regulares. The first battalion of 800 infantrymen and 100 horsemen was created in Melilla in 1911. In 1912 there were already two Tabors with 1,238 soldiers, and a third was created in Ceuta. In 1914 four Groups of Regulars (*Grupo de Regulares*) were organised, each with two infantry and a cavalry Tabor. In 1919 these Groups were called 1st of de Tetuán (from Melilla), 2nd of Melilla, 3rd of Ceuta and 4th of Larache. Each Tabor would have 122 Spanish and 341 Moroccan soldiers and officers. In August, a machine gun company was added, so that their firepower became greater than that of the line soldiers and the Cazadores: the latter had one machine gun company for every four or six companies, while the Regulares now had one for every three, and in addition they were smaller

four infantry and one cavalry due to the large number of Moors there sympathetic to Spain. Their uniform was very characteristic, with a red Fez or tarbuch (tarboosh) cap, a short zouave jacket, and wide, chickpea-coloured Moorish breeches. The cavalry troops wore turbans, as did all troops from 1922–1923. On the other hand, each one of the Groups wore a sash of a different colour, indigo blue for the 1st, red for the 2nd, light green for the 3rd, dark blue for the 4th, and amaranth red and then green for the 5th.[5]

Lieutenant Colonel Dámaso Berenguer Fusté, founder of the Regulares elite troops in 1911, a very capable man who become High Commissioner of Morocco (1919), Minister of War and then President of the Government of Spain in 1931, though he also suffered the Disaster of Annual. (via Gárate Córdoba)

A Regulares soldier in a studio picture. (via Carrasco and de Mesa)

Mehala Jalifian in action. Note the method of carrying their rifles. (via Carrasco and de Mesa)

Mehala Jalifian review in 1911. (via Carrasco and de Mesa)

Another native unit were the *Mehalas Jalifians*, created from 1913. These were entirely indigenous units, except for a cadre of instructors, which would serve as the basis for the future Royal Moroccan or Makhzen Army. In 1915 there were already six Mehalas of infantry and two of cavalry, with 110 soldiers for a Mía of infantry and 75 of those cavalry, then grouped in two Tabors. In

A Regulares soldier with the head of a Rifian rebel. According to some sources, in the Larache sector money was paid for each head of a rebel. One Moor asked for an extra amount as, allegedly, this was the head of his own father. (via Courcelle & Marmié)

1922 they began to incorporate all the survivors of the Indigenous Police after the disaster at Annual. The new Mehalas formed in 1923 consisted of three infantry Tabors and one cavalry Tabor each. The 1st Mehala was that of Tetouan; the 2nd of Melilla, the 3rd of Larache, the 4th of Xaouen (Xauén), dissolved in 1925, and the 5th of Tafersit. In 1926, based on the Harka of commander Capaz, the 6th Mehala of Gomara was formed, and the 4th Mehala, now called Yebala, was recreated. In 1925 there were already 5,230 Moroccan and 265 Spanish soldiers in nine Tabors and 48 Mías. They were very light units specially adapted for mountain warfare, without machine guns, only rifles and hand grenades, which shone especially in the campaigns of 1926 and 1927.[6]

Finally, there were other less prominent Moroccan units. The most brilliant were the irregular units of guerrillas allied to Spain, called friendly *Harkas*, at first under Moroccan commanders such as Abd el-Kader, but later under Spanish commanders such as Varela or Muñoz Grandes. Many of them amounted to 100-200 warriors, but the most powerful ones were around 1,000-1,500, which also gives us an idea of the limited war potential of the Rifians, rebels or not. These groups stood out above all during the Alhucemas landing in 1925 until the end of the war. More unecessary were the *Goums* and *Younds*, of French origin, irregular units of about 100 warriors, which hardly found an echo in Spain. Finally, the *Idalas* were a type of friendly Harkas but smaller and totally improvised, generally being a group of recently occupied kabyle people who offered to watch over their neighbours for the Spanish. They assisted the *Mezhanías*, a kind of Indigenous Police controlled by the so-called Offices of Intervention, in their control duties. The three Interventions created in 1925, of

Tetouan, Larache and Melilla, had a total of about 1,500 men, a third of them Spanish soldiers.[7]

The Spanish Legion

Friendship had much to do with the creation of the famous Spanish Legion or *Tercio de Extranjeros de la Legión*. Commander José Millán-Astray, an admirer of the French Foreign Legion, had in mind the creation of a similar elite corps in Spain, to have more reliable elements than the indigenous troops, who in theory could desert or even go over to the enemy. For him the ideal solution would be a corps of professional, volunteer and highly qualified soldiers, formed mainly by Spaniards, although open to other nationalities. In reality, foreigners accounted for about 17 percent, mostly Portuguese, Germans and Cubans. The project had the misgivings of the Spanish high command, which was not in favour of a professional army. Millán-Astray met Commander Francisco Franco at a shooting course in Madrid at the end of 1918, and both Galicians quickly became friends. In fact, Franco collaborated in the drafting of the Legion report prepared by Millán-Astray. To further develop the project, the commander was sent to Algeria and France and when he returned he obtained approval for the creation of the Legion on 4 September 1920. As second in command, Millán-Astray immediately counted on his friend Franco.

The units were organised in small battalions called *Banderas*, similar to the Tabors of the Regulares. Each one would have only three infantry companies of 200 soldiers, but in addition they would have another one of machine guns. Therefore, their firepower would be double that of the Cazadores and line infantry. Their uniforms were also different, to increase their *esprit de corps* and morale: jackets with turned-down collars, breeches with green puttees, Elizabethan caps with a tassel, leather boots and English Mills belts acquired in Gibraltar. Later, they used the *chambergo*, a large cloth hat more appropriate than the cap to protect the head from the sun. Its emblem was formed by a harquebus and a crossbow, reminiscent of the Flanders Tercios, and its moral code, the famous Legion Creed, was added. The first three Banderas were organised in 1920; at the end of 1921 the 4th and 5th, in September 1922 the 6th, in February 1925 the 7th, and in January 1926 the 8th Bandera.[8]

Their training and professionalism would make them a focus of attention for ambitious (in the best sense) and competent officers, although at an expensive price in blood: almost 50 percent of them were killed during the war. They would soon become the shock units of the Spanish army, ahead of even the Regulares. With such good soldiers it was easier for the officers to adopt more flexible deployments, forgetting the close order by companies and advancing now by sections, and even subdividing these into squads. In the same way, each individual soldier, better trained, knew how to solve situations by himself without waiting for orders: when and where to shoot, when to take cover in the terrain, when to advance, when to throw grenades, how to surround or enfilade the enemy, etcetera. In addition, in 1922 each company had its own heavy weapons section equipped with six Hotchkiss machine guns. By 1925 each section also had 60mm Lafitte mortars, which later were added to the heavy weapons company. In addition, the combat instructions were very precise. By way of example:

A unit must never stop in front of isolated shots of the enemy, whose purpose will be to slow down the march; the scouts, forming combat patrols, are in charge of driving the aggressors

A soldier of the Spanish Legion with his large campaign hat or *chambergo*. (via Marín Ferrer)

Lieutenant Colonel Millán-Astray, founder of the Spanish Legion, with his intimate friend Commander Franco, head of the 1st Bandera of the Legion. (Archivo General de la Administración, via Villalobos)

away. In front of the enemy or in his proximity, never pass a gorge without taking the heights that dominate it with flanking soldiers, which will join the rearguard once the force has passed. If you have to cross ravines, use the Frich system, not venturing in the pass without establishing yourselves in the height before the ravine, and to have set up small number of flankers on the right and left of the crossing point, crossing it then the forces that will establish in the same way on the other side their small posts, withdrawing under their protection the first ones established. The mobile flanks will try not to march along the same ridge in such a way that they can stand out over the horizon, their scouts being the only ones to march, if necessary, in this way.

The advance would be made by first organising a base of supporting fire with the heavy weapons company with which to distract and force the enemy to the ground. Meanwhile, two companies, in open order by sections and squads, would advance little by little, close to the ground, under cover, and trying to stay uncommitted and out of enemy fire as long as possible, followed by the third company as a reserve. When they were already close to the enemy the support fire had to cease, and as at that moment the Rifians used to counterattack, the advanced units would then throw hand grenades at them, and in the confusion of the explosions the Legion troopers would launch an assault, generally with knife and grenades, a moment that the Rifians avoided like the devil, fleeing. The orders and the coordination of these manoeuvres were made by means of whistles or visual signals with heliographs, waving arms or with pennants, which were frequently used for Morse code, which was obligatory to know. Often, there was no choice but to use messengers, which explains the very high percentage of casualties of these types of soldiers.[9]

The Spanish Deployments in Ceuta and Melilla

Having analysed the different types of Spanish troops, it is now possible to discuss the units that typically composed the garrisons and columns of the Spanish Protectorate in Morocco, later known as the Army of Africa. In principle, the units were grouped into two large units the size of a reinforced division: the Ceuta Command (that would also cover later the forces in Tetouan) and the Melilla Command. Later, around 1912–1913 the Larache Command would be created. It had in general less strength than the other commands, being instead equivalent to a reinforced brigade.

In principle, the Ceuta and Melilla Commands had two fixed line regiments each: the Ceuta and Serrallo Regiments for Ceuta, and the Melilla and África Regiments for Melilla, forming one infantry brigade in each command. The Melilla area had a 2nd Brigade made up of the Ceriñola and San Fernando Regiments until at least 1922. Then, the 1st and 2nd Melilla Infantry Brigades were reduced to just one, as in the Ceuta Command. In the Larache Command there was only an Expeditionary Marine Infantry Regiment, that later would disappear. In addition, the Ceuta and Melilla Command had a Cazadores Brigade each, since at least 1913 (the 1st and 2nd Cazadores Brigades), of four to six battalions in each brigade, subdivided into two Half Brigades. In Larache, there were only two Cazadores battalions, but later its forces were expanded to a full Cazadores Brigade, the 2nd, as in Ceuta, but at the expense of the Melilla Command which lost its Cazadores Brigade. Nevertheless, in the last years of the war, at least from 1926, every Command had six battalions of Cazadores, being the 1st to 6th in Ceuta, the 7th to 12th in Larache, and the 13th to 18th in Melilla.

Every command had a Cazadores cavalry regiment: the Taxdirt in Larache, the Vitoria in Ceuta, and the Alcántara in Melilla. In time the three commands each had a mixed or mountain artillery regiment, and an artillery command or coast and position artillery regiment. Finally, there was an engineer regiment each in Ceuta and Melilla, there being only an engineer battalion in Larache. Later, all commands were reduced to a mere battalion in each, as in 1926.

This more or less fixed force based permanently in Northern Morocco was completed with expeditionary line regiments, sometimes a mere battalion of a Peninsular regiment, but at others an entire line regiment. Also, there were the native troops (Regulares, Indigenous Police, Jalifian Mehalas and friendly Harkas), which were moved from area to area depending on the circumstances. There was more or less one Group of Regulares in Larache, two in Ceuta–Tetouan, and another in Melilla. Finally, the Spanish Legion was available from 1920, which was assigned to one area or another depending on the enemy activity. So, it began in the Tetouan area until the 1921 Disaster of Annual, when most of it was redeployed in Melilla. It was moved again in 1923–1924 to Tetouan to defend and then evacuate Xaouen, and finally again to the Melilla Command for the Alhucemas landing

and the final offensive in 1925–1926. In all, Spain began the war with some 20,000 men in Africa, and it reached a peak of some 125,000 soldiers from time to time.[10]

The Rifian Army

The Rif region roughly corresponded to the Spanish Protectorate, which covers an area of some 20,000 square kilometres. However, strictly speaking, not all of it was part of the Rif. In the west, the region around Ceuta and Tangier is known as La Yebala. Further south, around Larache, it is known as the Garb or Utauien or Lucus. Further east, there is the area of Gomara, with its capital in the holy city of Xaouen, and then there is the Rif proper, which extends to the river Kert. From here the region is sometimes known as the Eastern Rif or Kert, and finally the area around Melilla, in the far west, is known as the Guelaya. To the south of Guelaya there is an area of plains called Garet, the only terrain suitable for cavalry. The rest consists of a mountainous and very rugged area, with low but very steep hills and mountain ranges up to 2,000 metres high, and all this furrowed by gullies and dry riverbeds that are converted into natural trenches. This area, out of the governmental control of the Makhzen, had no higher organisation than the tribe or kabyle itself, which in turn was subdivided into sections. With a population of about 763,000 inhabitants divided into 70 kabyles (or 64 if the Senhaja Confederation is counted as just one kabyle as it controls seven tiny kabyles), each of these tribes had on average about 11,000 to 12,000 inhabitants. Of course, there were very large and densely populated kabyles, such as Beni Urriaguel (with about 65,000 inhabitants, the second largest of them all), Ajmas, Beni Buy Yahi or M'talsa, and other tiny ones such as those of the Senhaja. Therefore, in spite of the reports of the Spanish and French intelligence, its numerical potential was very low. The warlike potential of the Beni Urriaguels, the most powerful of all the kabyles, would not exceed 3,000 or 4,000 warriors; seven percent of the population. Probably Abd el-Krim, the most powerful of the rebels, counted about 14,500 warriors at hand in May 1926, and 29,000 in the whole Protectorate, uniting 37 kabyles and four half-kabyles. With notable exceptions, each rebel kabyle would contribute on average about 700 or 800 warriors, figures that have been used for this work.[11]

Of course, the Rifian warrior was an irregular and only had hunting weapons, bought by smuggling, or from native Spanish troops, but above all by those captured from their French and Spanish rivals, mainly after the Annual (1921) and the Ouarga (1925) offensives. These victories supplied them with about 18,000 rifles, about 250 machine guns, and above all 150 or 200 pieces of artillery. The largest armies were those of El Raisuni in the Yebala (1912–1925), which alternated confrontation with collaboration, or those of El Mizzián in the Guelaya (1909–1913), but none of them reached the power of Abd el-Krim (1921–1926). Abd el-Krim not only grouped together the great majority of the kabyles of the whole Protectorate, but also had artillery, machine guns and an incipient Rifian aviation of three aircraft, although none of them became operational. He expanded from his Beni Urriaguel kabyle throughout the central Rif, the Kert and almost all of the Guelaya. El-Krim then expanded throughout the Gomara and part of the Yebala and the Garb with the help of his brother M'hammed, an engineer trained in Spain, and El Jeriro, a former follower of El Raisuni. His total troops may have numbered some 29,000 warriors and although the great majority of them were still mere irregulars, Abd el-Krim began the construction of a regular army and the first institutions of a Rifian government. His

Rifian warriors mostly armed with single shot 11mm Remingtons, except for one who carries a Mauser 1916 across his back. (via Marín Ferrer)

them being captured in the Alhucemas landing.[12]

Rifian tactics have already been hinted at when talking about the Spanish army. It can be summarised in that the ambush was the most useful Rifian tactic, as well as attacking the wells and supply routes of the Spanish forces in their rear. They usually employed small parties, but sometimes several of them would join together to form a large Harka for an important offensive or to defend a place. Only at the end of the war, in the landing of Alhucemas in 1925, did the Rifians start to form tactical groupings of about 300 soldiers with two artillery pieces and three or four machine guns. Generally:

they made use of the smallest folds and accidents of the terrain to present a very thin front of sharpshooters, which made them very little vulnerable to artillery and rifle fire. They used both ridges and ravines as defensive positions … Once they saw the opportunity to go on the offensive, they used the ravines to move quickly, gaining the flank and rear of the enemy units so that shooting them from behind would cause their panic and disbandment.

They would shoot the enemy officers to leave the troops without their commanders. However, as mentioned above, they shunned close-range combat or the knife, fleeing when the Spaniards managed to get too close. They were capable of erecting improvised trenches, but with Abd el-Krim they even made European-style lines, using up to 3,000 troops at times.[13]

forces thus counted about 1,500 regular soldiers, artillerymen and 100 machine-gunners grouped in Tabors and Mías commanded by kaids, recruited among the six tribes of the central Rif: Beni Urriaguel, Bocoya, Temsaman, Beni Tuzin, Tafersit and Beni Ulixek. The Mías, numbering about 100 soldiers, even had uniforms: Abd el-Krim's personal guard of 200 men wore green on their turbans, red for the officers, blue for the troops and black for the artillerymen and machine-gunners. They were trained in European style, although their function, more than fighting, was to train and command the irregulars, to coordinate them, and to handle the heavy weapons. Also, they contracted several mercenaries, including a German veteran of the First World War, generally to handle the cannons and the machine guns, some of

2

1909 – The Gourougou Wasp Nest

The war began for Spain in 1909, and it would not end until 1927. Spain was counting on the forces and diplomacy of El Roghi, a rebel against the Sultan of Morocco, to peacefully expand its influence around Melilla. However, the failure of El Roghi in the central Rif, provoked a general uprising of the kabyles of the Guelaya, so that the Spanish mining activities in the area were suspended. Eight months later, in June, General Marina's Melilla garrison consisted of 5,547 men as detailed in Table 1.[1]

Table 1: Melilla Garrison (June 1909)
Melilla Infantry Regiment (three battalions)
África Infantry Regiment (three battalions)
Disciplinary Battalion (ex-convicts)
Melilla Cazadores Squadron
Two batteries (Melilla Artillery Command)
Mixed Company of sappers and Telegraphs
Sea Company

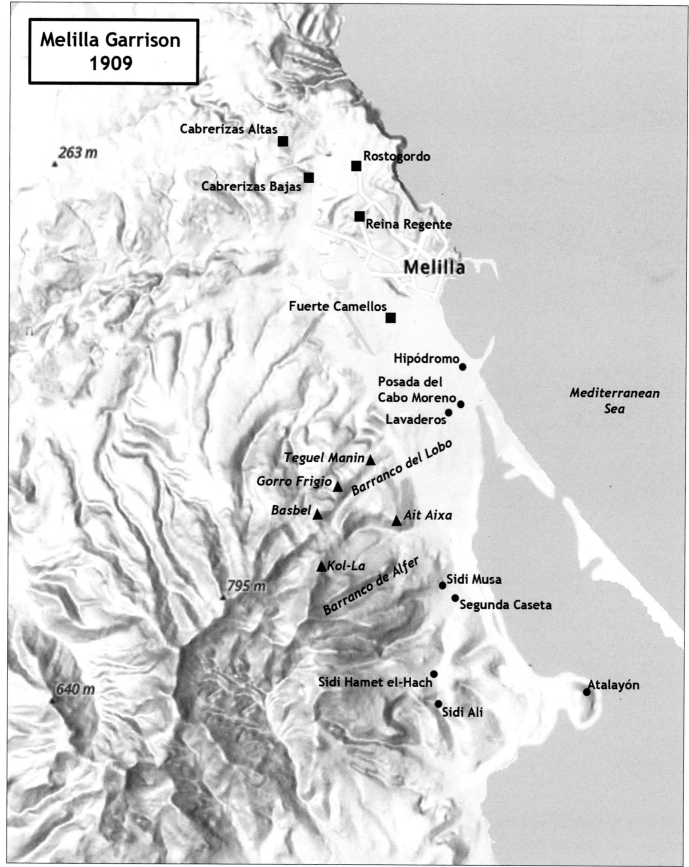

Melilla Garrison 1909

263 m

Cabrerizas Altas

Rostogordo

Cabrerizas Bajas

Reina Regente

Melilla

Fuerte Camellos

Hipódromo

Posada del Cabo Moreno

Lavaderos

Mediterranean Sea

Teguel Manin

Gorro Frigio

Barranco del Lobo

Basbel

Ait Aixa

Kol-La

Barranco de Alfer

Sidi Musa

Segunda Caseta

795 m

Sidi Hamet el-Hach

Atalayón

640 m

Sidi Ali

Map of the Melilla Region and the north-eastern side of Mount Gourougou in 1909. (Map by Tom Cooper, based on Villalobos)

After a period of relative calm, the Spanish mining companies recommenced their works on 11 June in the area of Mount Gourougou, some 20km south of Melilla, in the kabyle of Beni Bu Ifrur. However, their leaders, El Mizzián and El Chadly, again threatened the workers in the area, putting a gun to their foreman's head. To punish the rebels, on 3 July General Pedro del Real marched from La Restinga, a spit of land about 25km southeast of Melilla, with two infantry companies and several sections of machine guns, artillery and cavalry. Del Real seized cattle and rifles and took six prisoners after destroying several houses in the villages of the area (Charrauti, Zoco el Arbaa and Lehedara) but this action stirred up the spirits of the Rifians who, gathered

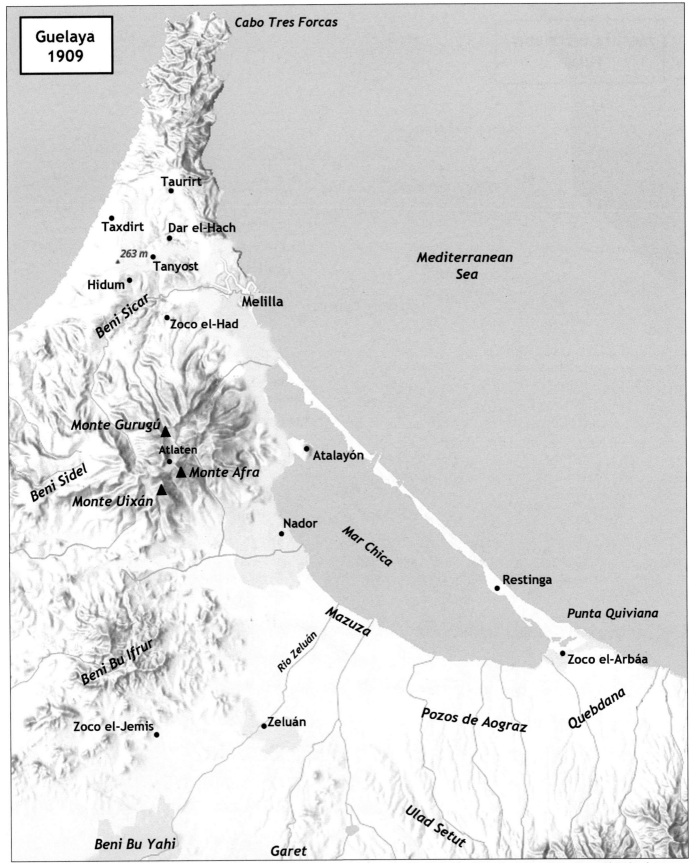

Map of the Guelaya in 1909, with Cape Tres Forcas (to the north, location of the battle of Taxdirt), Mar Chica (to the east), the Garet Plain (to the south), and Mount Gourougou. (Map by Tom Cooper, based on Villalobos, in turn based on C. Martínez de Campos's *España Bélica*, and T. Figueras's *Marruecos*)

in Mazuza, further west, planned new attacks for the 9th. From there, some 30 Rifians fired at the Spanish workers at the area east of the Gourougou, through the Sidi Musa ravine and killed six of them, barely 3km from Melilla. Lieutenant Colonel Enrique

Baños, hearing the shots, marched by train from the Hippodrome, on the southern outskirts of Melilla, with two companies of the África Infantry Regiment, to repel the rebels. Within an hour, General Marina himself set out with half the garrison of Melilla,

Soldiers building a well in Zoco el Arbaa. (via Gárate Córdoba)

Mohammed Amezian "El Mizzián", leader of the kabyle of Beni Bu Ifrur and of the Rifian rebellion of 1909–1912. (via Carrasco & de Mesa)

ominously above him, so he fortified his positions in the area and called for reinforcements. However, while these arrived, the Rifians, from the heights of the Gourougou, continued to shoot at the Spanish positions, causing between six and 10 casualties a day.[2]

On 16 July the 3rd Mixed Brigade of General Miguel de Imaz arrived at Melilla, coming from Barcelona. It was formed by the Cazadores battalions Alfonso XII, Barcelona, Estella, Reus, Alba de Tormes and Mérida, grouped in two Half Brigades. As a complement, the forces had two machine gun sections, the cavalry squadron of the Treviño Cazadores regiment, three batteries of mountain artillery, a company of sappers, another of telegraphs, and another of administration. This force added another 6,267 soldiers, so that the garrison of Melilla was doubled. In the meantime, the firing on the Spanish positions continued, and in addition it was detected that some 5,000 Rifians from Mazuza and other kabyles were marching along the road to Nador, south of the Gourougou, to help the rebels of Beni Bu Ifrur. Their attack fell on the Sidi Hamet positions on 18 July, just as the first Spanish reinforcements were beginning to relieve the troops stationed there by General Marina. The kabyle saw that the wall that was to close the right flank of the Spanish position was not yet finished, and they slipped through. Their defenders, still a mixture of África and Cazadores troops, fled to the redoubt, abandoning the artillery. There, Major José Royo and Captain Enrique Guiloche drew their revolvers and managed to defend the two Krupp pieces and the artillerymen, saving the cannons, but both were shot dead. After suffering 47 casualties, the Spaniards finally managed to repulse the Rifians. But the attacks continued and continued without Marina deciding to assault the Gourougou. On the 20th the positions of Sida Musa and the Segunda Caseta were attacked, and the Spaniards suffered 105 more casualties.[3]

Defeat at Barranco of Alfer

The hornet's nest of the Gourougou grew more and more, and already the Rifians dared on 22 July to expand the zones of their attacks, threatening the southern suburbs of Melilla, by shooting at Posada del Cabo Moreno, Lavaderos and the Hippodrome, to the north-east of the Gourougou. An enemy group was concentrated on the heights of Ait Aixa, to threaten from the north the Spanish positions in front of the Gourougou and to cut them off from Melilla. To prevent them from being enveloped, the Spaniards reacted, and after an artillery barrage that cleared Ait Aixa, a column formed by six companies and a mountain artillery section under Colonel Venancio Álvarez Cabrera was organised in the Hippodrome to drive the kabyles out. There are discrepancies as

some 2,500 troops in three battalions (including the Disciplinary Battalion) and a battery. Forming his troops in three separate columns, Marina carried out an enveloping action that ended up taking the heights of Barranco (ravine) of Sidi Musa (to the east of Mount Gourougou), Sidi Hamet el Hach and Sidi Ali, both to the south-east of this mountain, threatening to envelop it from the south. Next to Sidi Musa, a little further east, in the so-called Segunda Caseta (Second Hut), General Marina organised a supply depot, and occupied the port of Atalayon, further south-east, opposite Sidi Hamet and Sidi Ali, to improve his lines of communication by sea. The operations had cost him 31 casualties. Marina soon realised that to secure the mining works he would have to thoroughly occupy the Gourougou massif, which loomed

Spanish soldiers in La Restinga camp. (via Gárate Córdoba)

The *blocao* (blockhouse) Velarde in 1909, a typical defensive position around Melilla. (via Gárate Córdoba)

A convoy arriving at the Segunda Caseta Position, near Melilla. (via Gárate Córdoba)

the night, Cabrera began the ascent to the Gourougou to take Ait Aixa. At dawn on 23 July, perhaps lost in the darkness or perhaps trying to envelop the kabyle positions, Cabrera appeared on the right bank of the Ravine of Alfer. From there, exhausted by the night march, he retreated to the plain in front of the Sidi Musa post, to rest before making the attack. General Marina, aware of this, sent Captain Miguel Cabanellas (future rebel general in the Spanish Civil War) with orders to return to the Hippodrome, but he did not arrive in time. Thus, Cabrera was left alone on a plain below the Gourougou without the support of other forces, and all the fire of the thousands of Rifians was directed against him. In any case, the colonel was a brave man, and with about 100 soldiers from the África Regiment he marched to dislodge the Rifians before they could gain a foothold. The Moroccans retreated, went down the Ravine of Alfer and regrouped on the other side. Colonel Cabrera, imprudent, followed them, and when he entered the ravine he found that the Moroccans were waiting for him and when he ordered an assault he was killed after suffering 76 casualties. Only the fire from Sidi Musa's position managed to save the rest of his column. At the same time, nine more companies left the Hippodrome to form a line from there to Sidi Musa and support Cabrera's troops. Short of troops,

to whether Marina ordered Cabrera to attack directly or simply to wait for events, as he planned to occupy Ait Aixa with other forces, probably from the south, but the fact is that Cabrera immediately marched against those heights at 2200 hours. In the middle of

General Marina had to call in the first units of the new 1st Mixed Brigade from Madrid, which were disembarking precisely at that moment in Melilla. These troops, sent directly from the dock to the front, were the next victims: from the Hippodrome two companies of the Figueras Cazadores Battalion marched at 1000 hours under Lieutenant Colonel José Ibáñez Marín to the southern end of the Spanish line, near Sidi Musa, where they withstood enemy fire until 1700 hours. Then, General Marina considered the action finished after learning of the disaster suffered by Colonel Cabrera, and he ordered the withdrawal of all the forces from the Hippodrome. Lieutenant Colonel Ibáñez gave his troops, still recruits, some breathing space before leaving, at which point they were attacked: a group of Rifians came out of some cactus trees and cut the throats of the section that was on the guard, while another group came out of another nearby ravine and mowed down those who were resting. Surprised, the men of the Figueras Battalion fled, leaving the corpse of Colonel Ibáñez behind. In the end, Spain suffered 282 casualties that day. However, despite these setbacks, General Marina still held his positions around Melilla and around Sidi Musa, the area facing south-east of the Gourougou, although communications between the two groups of troops were precarious.[4]

Cazadores checking their Mausers in July 1909. (via Gárate Córdoba)

Mount Gourougou, with the Kol-la (1), Gorro Frigio or Taxit el Arbi (2) and Basbel (3) hills marked. (via Gárate Córdoba)

The Barranco del Lobo Disaster and the Tragic Week
General Marina continued to accumulate troops for his assault on the Gourougou, and as already mentioned, between 23 and 25 July the troops of the 1st Mixed Brigade from Madrid under General Guillermo Pintos Ledesma formed by the Madrid, Barbastro, Figueras, Arapiles, Las Navas and Llerena Cazadores battalions began to arrive at the Melilla docks. These forces were accompanied by a cavalry squadron of the Lusitania Cazadores Regiment, two companies of engineers, telegraphs, administration, and ambulances, and two groups of machine guns (two sections) and artillery of three 1878 Krupp batteries. With them, General Marina's forces now numbered 17,000 soldiers, and he was promoted to lieutenant general, while his old post was taken over by Major General Salvador Arizón. However, the arrival of these

Lieutenant Colonel Ibáñez Marín, Commander of the Figueras Battalion, killed in the Alfer assault. (via Marín Ferrer)

A Cazadores machine gun section arriving at Melilla. Note the Ros caps with their neck cover. (via Marín Ferrer)

reinforcements came at a very high cost. The decree of Antonio Maura's government was to send reserve troops to the Spanish possessions in Morocco, most of these being working class men. The trade unions called for a general strike that ended in a revolt in Barcelona between 26 July and 2 August: the famous *Semana Trágica* (Tragic Week). The workers blocked the streets with barricades, set fires, especially in churches, lynched, committed some murders, and even formed Revolutionary Councils and proclaimed a republic in some Catalan cities. The repression was also very harsh, with 1,700 arrested. In addition, 441 people were injured, and 104 civilians and eight military personnel were killed.

Meanwhile, the Spanish forces to the south, in front of the Gourougou, were threatened with envelopment. More and more bonfires could be seen in the bush and at night the kabyles managed to slip through and lift the railway tracks that ran from Melilla to the Segunda Caseta. To reopen communications and supply these forces, Lieutenant General Marina sent a convoy escorted by a column under Colonel Juan Fernández Cuerda, consisting of six infantry companies, one of engineers, a squadron, and a section of artillery. Its advance to the south would be covered by the entire 1st Brigade of General Pintos, who would watch from the Hippodrome to ensure that no Rifian forces came out to attack the convoy. The convoy, although shot at, managed to repair the railway lines. Meanwhile, General Pintos, further north, advanced to the foothills of the Gourougou, attracting enemy fire to help the convoy, but then disaster struck. The Rifians were concentrating on the north face of the Gourougou. General Pintos, from his position, thought that the hills ascended gently, but he did not know that several transversal ravines cut his line of advance. Thus, after counting on an artillery barrage, he marched with a line of five battalions from Lavaderos (the mineral washes), leaving the sixth one, Figueras, in reserve. On the extreme right of the line (to the west) the Madrid Battalion advanced, occupying some bluffs, and three companies of the Barbastro Battalion went still further to the right to cover its flank, forming a new line at right angles. General Pintos was on horseback in the vanguard, together with a line of skirmishers, close to those of the Madrid Battalion. However, when he came down for a moment to rest, a shot struck

his head and killed him barely 1km from Lavadero. With his fall and due to the heavy fire, the whole right line came to a halt. Meanwhile, on the other side of the line (to the east), the battalions Las Navas, Llerena and Arapiles, under Colonel Páez Jaramillo, were able to cross the Infierno (Hell) Ravine, but due to the obstacles of the terrain, they were crowding towards the centre of the formation, entering Lobo (Wolf) Canyon. Due to lack of space, the Las Navas Battalion penetrated first, followed by the Llerena Battalion. There, the Rifians delivered massive fire from both flanks and the front but, crowded together, the Spaniards could not retreat, and were pushed by the troops coming behind, as the ravine progressively narrowed. The officers, 10 from Navas and 17 from Llerena, who were always in the open to set an example, were massacred. Lieutenant Colonel Palacios, an example for his men, also fell, causing them to disband. A vanguard of 40 soldiers under Lieutenant Joaquín Tourné, from Las Navas, tried to take the heights, but they were annihilated with their officer: 30 of them fell. Nevertheless, their action held back the Rifians, giving the Spaniards some breathing space, who then began to retreat. At this point the first elements of Llerena arrived, which formed a defensive angle to cover the retreat of Las Navas, but they were also overwhelmed, and so Colonel Páez Jaramillo ordered the Arapiles Battalion to enter the ravine at the bayonet to dislodge the Rifians. Lieutenant General Marina, who was observing the advance from Lavaderos, had already noticed that the line of march of the Madrid Brigade was heading for disaster, so he ordered the advance to be rectified, but the messenger with the order arrived too late. Even so, the general managed to rearrange the line of battle and withdraw his troops, covered by the convoy escort, after suffering 762 casualties. The Rifians, according to Spanish estimates, had suffered between 100 and 475 casualties. In the end, Lieutenant General Marina returned to his starting positions, with two groups of forces, leaving the southern ones half isolated again, and waiting for new reinforcements to break the Gourougou nut.[5]

An Army of Three Divisions

Lieutenant General Marina, chastened after the setbacks of July, decided not to carry out any more attacks until he was duly reinforced. On 31 July the 2nd Mixed Brigade of Campo de Gibraltar, under General José Morales, landed in Melilla. The unit was made up of the Cataluña, Tarifa, Ciudad Rodrigo, Segorbe, Chiclana and Talavera Cazadores battalions, a squadron of the Alfonso XII Cazadores Regiment, as well as an artillery group, a machine gun group, and the same support companies as the other Cazadores brigades. Therefore, Marina's forces now numbered 22,000 soldiers. But that was not all, as between 3 and 9 August the 1st Reinforced Organic Division of General Gabriel Orozco disembarked, formed by two brigades: the 1st,

The "Urano" balloon, spherical type, being observed by the Rifians. (via Sánchez & Kindelán)

General Aguilera, commander of the 1st Brigade/1st Reinforced Division. (via Gárate Córdoba)

under General Francisco Aguilera, with the 1st Inmemorial Del Rey[6] and 38th León regiments; and the 2nd, under General Francisco San Martín, with the 6th Saboya (Savoy) and 50th Wad Ras regiments, both with machine gun groups. As support forces, the division had two squadrons of the María Cristina Cazadores Regiment, three artillery batteries and other support units, totalling 8,500 men. With all these troops, Marina organised his forces into the 1st Division of Orozco already mentioned; the Cazadores Division of General Antonio Tovar (with the 1st Cazadores Brigades of Madrid, now under General Felipe Alfau, and 2nd Gibraltar); the 3rd Cazadores Brigade of Barcelona, and the garrison Brigade of Melilla, of General del Real, together with the Disciplinary Battalion. But in addition, on 12 August three squadrons of the Princess Hussars Regiment arrived in the city, and between 5 and 14 September, the 2nd Organic Division of General Fernando Álvarez de Sotomayor, with the 1st Brigade (Príncipe no. 3 and Burgos no. 36 regiments) and 2nd Brigade (Cuenca no. 27 and Guipúzcoa no. 53 regiments), each of them with only one machine gun section, and two or three squadrons of the Alfonso XIII Cazadores Regiment. Thus, with the arrival of this unit, Lieutenant General Marina would have about 44,000 soldiers grouped in three divisions and two brigades. Also, the air force also made its debut when the Air Station Company, formed by the captive balloons *Reina Victoria* (a kite type), and *Urano* (spherical), joined the expedition.[7]

Now, however, Lieutenant General Marina decided to first clear all the areas surrounding the Gourougou, in order, once isolated, to launch his final conquest. He would begin with the Quebdana area, south-east of Melilla, next to the border with French Morocco. This region had been generally loyal to Spain but was already beginning to have dissident sections in the kabyle, so a campaign was planned. This planning should have been a model for others due to its effectiveness, but sadly it was easily forgotten. The Quebdana was to be attacked by two converging columns: the smaller, under Colonel Francisco Larrea, was sent by sea to Cabo de Agua, at the eastern end of the Spanish Protectorate, and from there it would advance westwards. Larrea had three companies, a section of machine guns and some cavalry and knew the area perfectly well, as well as having friends among the kabyles, so everything went smoothly. On 26 August at Tasaguin he defeated some 300 Rifians who were harassing the garrison at Cabo de Agua and advanced as far as the Muluya river. Then, between 3 and 9 September, he was reinforced with 800 soldiers from the Indigenous Police and 200 Rifians from a friendly Harka under the Kaid Ben Checha, and he explored the whole area between the Muluya and the coast, burning the houses of the rebels and seizing weapons, to then return along the coast to Melilla. At the same time, from the west, another larger column supported it, that of General Aguilera, who, with elements of the 1st Brigade/1st Division (the Inmemorial del Rey Regiment and two squadrons of cavalry) left La Restinga (on the spit of land that joins Melilla with the Quebdana), occupying Zoco el Arbaa, south-east of the Mar Chica, and reinforced with the León Regiment expelled a Harka that was harassing the town of Lehedara. General Aguilera, after clearing the entire east coast of the Mar Chica (Little Sea) and supporting the Larrea column, ended up returning to Lehedara, which was destroyed by artillery as the town had changed sides. Thus, in a campaign of about two weeks, the whole of Quebdana was brought under control very effectively. Spain used smaller but more mobile and agile columns, which always advanced in enemy territory, without retreating, with the help of large native

Table 2: The Army in Melilla (August – October 1909)		
Cazadores Division (General Antonio Tovar)	1st Mixed Brigade of Madrid (General Guillermo Pintos, later General Felipe Alfau)	Madrid, Barbastro, Figueras, Arapiles, Las Navas, Llerena Cazadores battalions
		Cavalry Squadron Lusitania Cazadores Regiment
		3 Batteries
	2nd Mixed Brigade of Gibraltar (General José Morales)	Cataluña, Tarifa, Ciudad Rodrigo, Segorbe, Chiclana, Talavera Cazadores battalions
		Cavalry Squadron Alfonso XII Cazadores Regiment
		Artillery Group
		Machine Gun Group
	3rd Mixed Brigade of Barcelona (General Miguel de Imaz)	Alfonso XII, Barcelona, Estella, Reus, Alba de Tormes, Mérida Cazadores battalions
		Cavalry Squadron Treviño Cazadores Regiment
		3 Batteries
1st Reinforced Division (General Gabriel Orozco)	1st Brigade (General Francisco Aguilera)	1st Inmemorial del Rey Regiment (3 battalions)
		38th León Regiment (three battalions)
		Artillery Group
	2nd Brigade (General Francisco San Martín)	2nd Saboya Regiment (3 battalions)
		50th Wad Ras (3 battalions)
		Machine Gun Group
	Support	2 Squadrons María Cristina Cazadores Regiment
		3 Batteries
2nd Organic Division (General Fernando Álvarez de Sotomayor) (September)	1st Brigade	3rd Príncipe Regiment (3 battalions)
		36th Burgos Regiment (three battalions)
	2nd Brigade	27th Cuenca Regiment (three battalions)
		53rd Guipúzcoa Regiment (3 battalions)
	Support	2 to 3 Squadrons Alfonso XIII Cazadores Regiment
	Independent Melilla Garrison Brigade (General Pedro Del Real)	África Infantry Regiment (3 battalions)
		Melilla Regiment (3 battalions)
		Cavalry Squadron Melilla Cazadores Regiment
3rd Organic Division (General Luis Huertas Urrutia) (October)	1st Brigade (General Carbó)	Ceriñola no. 42 Regiment (3 battalions)
		San Fernando no. 11 Regiment (3 battalions)
	1st Cavalry Brigade (General Milans del Bosch)	Hussars of the Princess (3 squadrons), Pavía cavalry regiments
Support		Disciplinary Battalion
		Hussars of the Princess, (replaced in October by Lanceros de la Reina) cavalry regiments

forces, knowing the terrain, counting on allies in the area, and practising scorched earth tactics in hostile areas, burning houses and harassing the enemy in their territory until, exhausted, they were forced to retreat or surrender. Unfortunately, these lessons were soon forgotten.[8]

Cavalry Charge at Taxdirt

Once the Quebdana was controlled, and Lieutenant General Marina was reinforced with his three divisions, he resumed the offensive, this time towards the north of Melilla, to control Beni Sicar's kabyle, which had been sending warriors to the Gourougou mountains. On 20 September General Tovar's Cazadores, Sotomayor's 2nd Division, and Del Real's Melilla Brigade, departed against Beni Sicar. The rookies of the 2nd Division were left as a reserve at Rostrogordo. From there, Tovar's Cazadores advanced to Dar el Hach Bisiain, further north at the base of the Tres Forcas Peninsula. Between the Cazadores and Melilla remained Del Real's troops (six companies and three batteries), covering the line of communications.[9] In front of them there were two large concentrations of Rifians: one to the south, at Zoco el-Had, keeping an eye on the 2nd Division, and another further north, at Tafarart, defending the area of the Cazadores. These ones, specifically the 1st Mixed Cazadores Brigade (4,029 men and eight pieces), under General Alfau and with Lieutenant General Marina himself, broke away from Tovar's division and advanced further north, encountering little resistance until reaching Taourirt. From there they marched to the sea, contacting the fleet that had sailed from Melilla and was waiting for them on the western coast of Cape Tres Forcas. At the same time, the 2nd Mixed

General Larrea returning to Melilla after pacifying the right side of the Muluya River. (via Gárate Córdoba)

A sentinel at a forward post in Beni Sicar. (via Gárate Córdoba)

Brigade of Cazadores (3,479 men and eight pieces), under General Morales, with General Tovar himself, turned west from Dar el Hach to reach the plateau of Taxdirt, and from there to the south towards the village of that name which was taken by a cavalry patrol. There, General Tovar discovered that the Hendok ravine lay between them and the heights of Tamsyut or Tanyost, further

south. Tamsyut was on the rebel left, where a new line of Rifians from Zoco el-Had had been formed, and at the same time, the other group of kabyle from Beni Sicar were still concentrated in Tafarart, on the right. This second group was threatening the left flank of the Spanish cavalry, located in the vanguard. To clear the frontal threat, General Tovar sent the Cataluña Battalion under Lieutenant Colonel Severiano Martínez Anido, who in a bayonet charge expelled the Rifians from Tamsyut. But the Moors had only moved a little further south-east, in the hills of Hidum,

A painting by Eduardo Banda showing the Spanish charge at Taxdirt. (via Gárate Córdoba)

Cavalcanti's riders beginning the cavalry charge at Taxdirt. (via Gárate Córdoba)

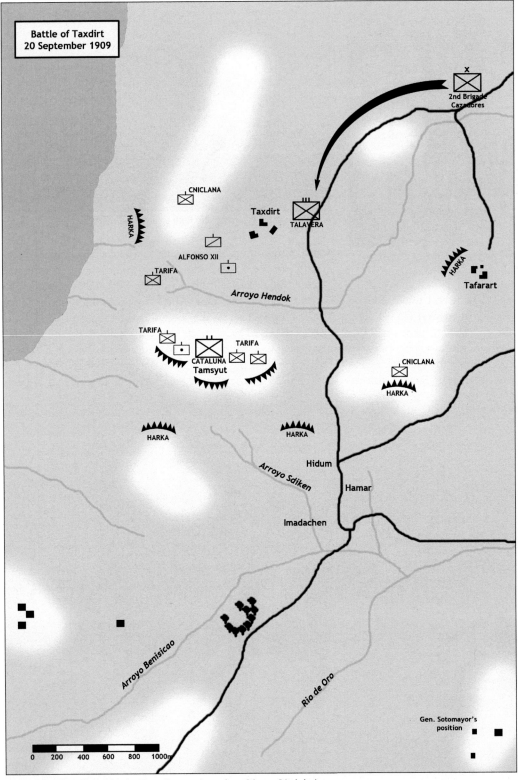

The battle of Taxdirt. (Map by Tom Cooper, based on Gárate Córdoba)

José Cavalcanti. This squadron, with only 65 horsemen, started from the rear, in Taxdirt, trotted down the Hendok ravine and went up it again, moving to a reed bed that hid them from the sight of the Moors. Cavalcanti charged then, sabre in hand, with his squadron against the first line of Rifians threatening Tamsyut, with one platoon to the front and the others to the right, or also to the left according to some sources. The Moors shot at point-blank range but then disbanded, managing to join a second line already formed by some 1,000 or 1,500 warriors. Cavalcanti regrouped his forces, now 40 horsemen, leaving the corpses and wounded in the cane field and charged the second line again before the Moors were able to consolidate, dispersing them. And again Cavalcanti, now with 20 horsemen, took advantage of the momentum and continued his charge, this time partly from the front and partly turning on the right flank over several groups of scattered Moors. However, by now the Spaniards were too few and here the Rifians held out, so the squadron dismounted and took cover on a rise behind the reed beds until a company of the Tarifa Battalion reached them. Thus, the charge of Taxdirt entered into legend, since this handful of men after suffering 24 casualties, including seven dead, saved the whole brigade from defeat. For this action Cavalcanti was decorated with the Laureate Cross of San Fernando 2nd Class (*Cruz Laureada de San Fernando* or the Laureate, the highest medal in Spain) and the whole squadron received the Tie of the same Order.

The Tarifa Battalion then charged with the bayonet and occupied the reed bed, driving the Moors beyond the Sdiken stream, behind Hidum hill. The Rifians, however, numbering 5,000 or 6,000 warriors, were still on the field, and continued firing against the 2nd Brigade. General Morales, with his troops overextended between Taxdirt and Tanyost and without reserves, called for reinforcements, but they did not arrive, so he began to fall back towards the plateau, to Taxdirt, while his artillery fired shrapnel shells at point-blank range to hold back the waves of

from where they tried to envelop Tamsyut and recover it. Seeing Cataluña's left flank in the air, they began to fire on it, so General Tovar began to deploy all his companies to Cataluña's left and right, to cover it. After four or five hours of shooting, Cataluña began to abandon the heights of Tamsyut for ammunition and rest, being relieved by those of the Tarifa Battalion. At that moment the Beni Sicar attacked, when only one isolated Cataluña company was left covering the retreat and almost out of ammunition, and before the Tarifa units had arrived. With this unit about to be surrounded, General Tovar sent to its help the 4th Cavalry Squadron of the Alfonso XII Regiment under his assistant, Lieutenant Colonel

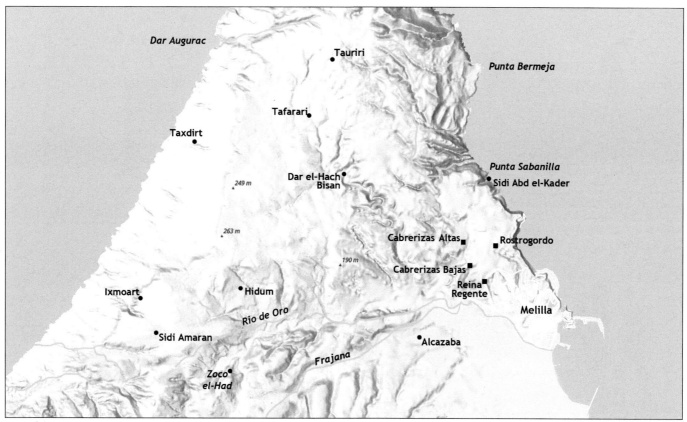

Map of the Cape Tres Forcas and Taxdirt area. (Map by Tom Cooper, based on Gárate Córdoba)

Another view of Cavalcanti's charge, climbing a hill, showing the rugged terrain. (via Gárate Córdoba)

General Antonio Tovar, commander of the Cazadores Division, who fought at Taxdirt. (via Gárate Córdoba)

General Tovar, of the Cazadores Division, with his son Captain Tovar, and his assistant, Lieutenant Colonel Cavalcanti, who was sent to lead the charge at Taxdirt. (via Gárate Córdoba)

Spanish mountain artillery in the Taxdirt area. Note the Wolseley salacots of the artillerymen. (via Gárate Córdoba)

Spanish artillery of Tovar's division in the Taxdirt area. Note the mix of Ros caps and barracks caps. (via Gárate Córdoba)

Hasmani "El Gato" (the Cat), leader of a friendly Harka, talking with Spanish soldiers and civilians. (via Gárate Córdoba)

General Morales, commander of the 2nd Cazadores Brigade. (via Gárate Córdoba)

A wounded soldier being attended to after the battle of Taxdirt. (via Gárate Córdoba)

its left flank, covered by the friendly Harka of Asmani "el Gato" (the Cat). General Sotomayor occupied the Zoco. Then, on the dawn of the 28th, he suffered a strong attack against his camp, but it was the last one in this sector. In this action, Corporal Luis Noval Terros was captured and forced by the Rifians to show them the holes in the barbed wire and the sign, but when approaching the Spanish lines, Noval Terros shouted: 'Make fire, I am with the Moors', and therefore he was shot by his comrades, but this ended the surprise attack by the Moors. He received the Laureate 2nd Class.

With all of Beni Sicar cleared, Tovar's Cazadores Division returned to Melilla, leaving two battalions guarding Taourirt. The operations had cost 161 Spanish casualties, but, unbeknownst to them, Lieutenant General Marina had at last succeeded in getting the Rifians to abandon the Gourougou and to battle on more or less open ground, suffering a serious defeat. The Gourougou had been practically empty, from which can be deduced that the Rifians had moved from there and concentrated their forces in Taxdirt (hence their large numbers) to try to save Beni Sicar's forces but without success.[10]

Rifians. Then troops of the 2nd Division arrived as reinforcements from the south, as well as two battalions of Alfau's 1st Cazadores Brigade from the north. Thus, the Spaniards held from the night of the 20th until the 21st in their lines, and on the 22nd they resumed the offensive. General Morales advanced with his brigade to the south-west of Taxdirt to take the heights of Hidum, while all of Sotomayor's 2nd Division advanced against Zoco el-Had, enveloping the entire northern slope of the Gourougou with

Neutralising the Gourougou

While Lieutenant General Marina cleared the accesses from the north of the Gourougou, in the southern part the Spaniards continued their slow approach from the Mar Chica and Quebdana. Orozco's 1st Division, with its 1st and 2nd Brigades of Aguilera and San Martín, in Zoco el Arbaa and Punta Quiviana respectively, were at the end of the tongue of land that separates the Mar Chica from the Mediterranean. Opposite was the plain of Bu Areg, the next objective of the Spanish forces. The hot air balloons ascertained the absence of rebel forces, so the division advanced south to the Aograz Pits on 20 September, being reinforced by the Princesa squadrons. The 1st Division then turned to its right and crossing the Selouane River marched north, taking the so-called Tetas de Nador (Tits of Nador, due to the appearance of the two hills surrounding the town) and its village, at the cost of only 11 wounded. It seemed evident that the bulk of the Rifians were at that time concentrated to the north, at the battle of Taxdirt, due to the little resistance offered. Once the Taxdirt battle ended, Lieutenant General Marina moved to Nador together with Tovar's Cazadores Division, and with Orozco's 1st Division. They advanced again to the south, this time against Selouane on 27 September. General Tovar advanced from the interior, near the Beni Ifrur mountains, and General Orozco from the coast, to then go up the river and reach the town of Selouane, which they did the same day, only hindered by sporadic fire on Tovar's flank.

Meanwhile, further north, in Melilla itself, seeing the absence of enemy fire, General Arizón made an incursion into the Gourougou, arriving at Lobo Canyon with three companies of the Navas Battalion on 28 September, recovering 108 Spanish corpses that had been there for two months. The next day, Arizón coordinated the final offensive to occupy the Gourougou: on the right or north, Lieutenant Colonel Luis Aizpuru, followed by Lieutenant Colonel Bermúdez de Castro's column, took Teguel Manin, and then climbed the mountain of Basbel. On his left, Colonel Ignacio Axó with the África Regiment ascended the Kol-la peak from Sidi Musa. And finally, in the centre, Colonel Miguel Primo de Rivera took Ait Aixa and Gorro Frigio, heights overlooking Lobo Canyon. From there the Spanish command understood that the hill of Ait Aixa was the key to the whole Gourougou, since from there Moors could see the whole plain of Melilla, could monitor all the Spanish movements, and shoot at them at will. If the first attack planned by Lieutenant General Marina on Ait Aixa at the beginning of July had been carried out correctly and without the impetuosity of Colonel Cabrera, Spain would have won the war in a few days and would have saved hundreds of dead. However, the

Lieutenant Colonel Bermúdez de Castro gives instructions to commander Berenguer. (via Gárate Córdoba)

Cazadores in the Caballo River Valley, from Tauima, with Selouane and El Afra behind. (via Gárate Córdoba)

Soldiers of the Disciplinary Battalion and the Aizpuru column crowning Mount Basbel, Gourougou. (via Gárate Córdoba)

Soldiers of the Melilla Regiment climb to the top of Mount Aixa. (via Gárate Córdoba)

Spanish command still did not entirely learn the lesson: little by little the Rifians returned to the Gourougou area, probably from the Taxdirt zone, and General Arizón ordered the withdrawal of Axó and Aizpuru's columns in the afternoon, so that Spain lost again all the conquered positions except the Gorro Frigio and Ait Aixa. In the retreat, the friendly Harka that covered the march was isolated and enveloped, suffering many casualties. In spite of everything, the Gourougou was partially neutralised, since from Ait Aixa all the accesses from Melilla were controlled, so that the operation was a great achievement, celebrated in all of Spain as a milestone to the coming end of the war.[11]

The Setback of Zoco El Jemís

The Rifian Harka apparently moved further south in an attempt to recapture Selouane. To protect the town, Lieutenant General Marina sent two battalions and two batteries from the Buguensein post, a stronghold that guarded the mountainous area. At the same time, on 30 September, eight battalions of Cazadores from Tovar's division advanced to explore Zoco El Jemís, further west, the main market of Beni Bu Ifrur. The advance was covered by the 2nd Brigade of Orozco's 1st Division, under the newly arrived General Díez Vicario, who had replaced San Martín. About 6km from Selouane, the Cazadores Division began to receive fire on its left flank. Two companies of the Llerena Battalion were sent to support the cavalry to cover this sector, and the Madrid Battalion was left covering them on some high ground. The bulk of the Rifians, formed by the kabyles of Beni Bu Ifrur, Beni Sidel and M'talsa, were concentrated in the central part, in front of Zoco El Jemís, on some hills. The vanguard was made up of the 2nd Mixed Brigade of Cazadores, with two companies of the Cataluña Battalion, the mountain battery of Captain Hernández Herce in the centre, and on the right the Ciudad Rodrigo Battalion. Cavalcanti, the hero of Taxdirt, marched with them. They scouted the enemy lines with the Alfonso XIII Regiment, suffering 11 casualties but reporting the size of the enemy forces. The enemy tried to envelop the Spanish line on the flanks, which forced Tovar to deploy companies to the ends of his line, leaving the centre weaker, so he requested the reinforcement of the 2nd Brigade of Darío Díez Vicario, while initiating the withdrawal. This movement exalted the Rifians, who launched an attack and occupied the heights that the Spaniards were abandoning. The Spaniards had to stop on several occasions and repulse the Rifians by bayonet to be able to continue the retreat. At that moment Vicario's 2nd Brigade arrived and set up to cover the retreat, while the Cazadores finally abandoned the front line. Then, having accomplished his mission, General Vicario began the retreat of his unit, when a bullet hit him in the chest. Colonel Luis Aranda then took command and managed to withdraw the brigade, although harassed and with heavy casualties. However, during the retreat, Captain Herce's battery, following

Vicario's orders, had been left containing the Rifians with its cannon fire, was isolated. As the general's permission to begin the retreat did not reach him, Herce was left alone against the Rifians until he finally received the order to retreat, at which point he made an impressive retreat by sections, each of them successively covering the retreat of the other without losing a single man. In any case, Herce's action was a poor consolation, as the Spaniards lost 307 men in this action.[12]

The Final Push to the Gourougou

In October, new reinforcements arrived for Lieutenant General Marina; the cavalry regiments Húsares de Pavía, Lanceros de la Reina (Lancers of the Queen) and the 1st Brigade of the new 3rd Organic Division, under General Fernando Carbó (formed by the Regiments Ceriñola no. 42 and San Fernando no. 11). On 17 October, operations were resumed to occupy the Beni Bu Ifrú mountains, where the main mining area that had been the cause of the conflict was located. By this time, the war was extremely unpopular in Spain because of the bloody setbacks and the impression that the children of the workers were being sent to their death to protect the interests of mining capitalism, and the government was desperate to get out of it. Thus, remembering the Tragic Week of Barcelona, operations slowed down. In the southern sector, a column under General Aguilera formed from elements of the 1st Brigade of the 1st Division, reconnoitred the Iksane valley, through the Atlaten area, with the help of an observation balloon. The next day, further south, some fighting took place on the banks of the Selouane River, in which the balloon camp was shot at, and where the Rifians were repulsed. There was then a new halt in the operations when the envoys of the Sultan tried to make the rebels accept Spanish rule and, at the same time, the conservative government of Maura fell and was replaced by the liberals of Moret. On 6 November, in the northern sector, the Spaniards occupied Hidum, in the area of Beni Sicar, near Taxdirt, and the following day Teguel Manin, to the south, in the north-eastern area of the Gourougou. Both positions had been taken by Spain in September but had been abandoned. Finally, on 26 November, the final offensive began in the southern sector with 17,816 troops. These forces consisted of: General Tovar's Cazadores Division, with General Morales' 1st Mixed Brigade (the

Spanish troops celebrate the taking of Mount Gourougou. (via Marín Ferrer)

Cazadores battalions of Cataluña, Segorbe, Chiclana, Talavera and Tarifa, a squadron of the Regiment Lanceros de la Reina, and two mountain batteries of Campo de Gibraltar) and the 2nd Brigade of General Enrique Brualla (the Burgos Regiment, a battalion of the Príncipe (Prince's) Regiment, the Barbastro Cazadores battalion, a squadron of the Alfonso XIII Regiment and three artillery batteries); General Diego Muñoz Cobo's Division, formed by General Juan López Herrero's 1st Brigade (the Saboya and Wad Ras Regiments, two squadrons of the María Cristina Regiment, and three batteries), and General Modesto Navarro García's 2nd Brigade (the 1st Inmemorial Del Rey Regiment, Barcelona and Mérida Battalions, a squadron of the Treviño Regiment and two batteries); and the Division of General Luis Huertas Urrutia, formed by the 1st Cavalry Brigade of General Milans del Bosch (the Hussars of the Princesa and Pavía Regiments) and the 2nd Brigade of General Carbó (the San Fernando Regiment, two companies of the Melilla Regiment, two others from the África Regiment, the Disciplinary Battalion and a battery).

These troops left Nador to envelop the Gourougou from its southern slope, taking Atlaten, Sebt and Segangan. Once these operations ended, the war also finished on the 27th. Progressively, the Spanish troops repatriated until August 1910. In the end, with difficulty, Spain had managed to regain control of the mining areas near Melilla, as well as Cape Tres Forcas, the Mar Chica and Bu Areg, with the submission of the kabyles of Quebdana, Beni Sicar, Beni Bu Gafar, Beni Bu Yahi, Ulad Settut, Mazuza, Beni Sidel and Beni Bu Ifrur, some 5,000 Rifian warriors in all. However, to do so it had had to mobilise up to 50,000 men and had lost some 7,000 soldiers: 259 killed in action, 200 more from disease, 1,523 wounded and 5,142 sick. On the other hand, El Mizzián was still alive, and although his kabyle of Beni Bu Ifrur had been occupied, he was able to cross the Kert to the west, in the central Rif, with some of his people and seek refuge in M'talsa, the most populous kabyle in the Rif, led by Hach Amar. And this was just a foretaste of what the Rif War would imply for Spain …[13]

3
1911–1912: The Kert River Campaign

In June 1910, the Spanish government fixed the contingent of the new Captaincy General of Melilla at 20,500 men (all line troops except three battalions of Cazadores of the 2nd Mixed Brigade, which were not repatriated). Lieutenant General Marina, much criticised for the previous campaign, was replaced by General José García Aldave, who had some experience coming from the Military Government of Ceuta. Aldave's first actions were to try to occupy the borders of the Spanish Protectorate before the French moved forward. Therefore, the newly promoted General Larrea marched to take the kabyle of Ulad Settut, until he reached the outpost of Zaio on 15 May, in front of the theoretical French line. The vanguard, formed by a battalion of the Melilla Regiment, was followed by three reserve columns, those of General Orozco, Colonel Astilleros, of the San Fernando Regiment, and that of Lieutenant Colonel Bermudez Dorado. For his part, El Mizzián met with the Spanish general and promised his support, but the rebel warrior disappeared very soon.[1]

García Aldave then had to shift his attention eastwards to the river Kert, as the fled El Mizzián had convinced Hach Amar of M'talsa, at the source of the Kert, south-west of Melilla, to join the holy war against Spain. The neighbouring kabyle of Beni Bu Yahu, just south of the Gourougou and adjacent to the subdued Beni Bu Ifrur of the exiled El Mizzián, would also join. These kabyles were soon joined by those of the central Rif, on the other side of the river Kert: Temsaman, Beni Urriaguel (the most bellicose and the second most populous of the Rif, with some 65,000 inhabitants) and Bocoya. As for their armament, it was known that at the end of 1909 a Dutch ship had smuggled a cargo of 8,000 rifles, 1,000 revolvers and a million cartridges, a good indication of the potential strength of the rebels. The neighbouring kabyles, Beni Bu Gafar and Beni Sedil, along the eastern bank of the Kert, began to be harassed by the rebels, so they asked the Spaniards for protection. To prevent these forces from crossing the Kert, García Aldave sent two columns up the river. One column went from north to south, in Yanazen (Beni Bu Gafar kabyle), next to the sea. The other column departed from Atlaten, in Beni Sidel, south

Captain General of Melilla José García Aldave, commander of Ceuta in 1909, he led the Kert campaign in 1911–1912 until the death of El Mizzián. (Gárate Córdoba)

Kaid Hach Amar of M'talsa, a kabyle placed at the source of the Kert, who was convinced by El Mizzián to confront the Spaniards in 1911–1912. Later he became allied to Spain, at least in 1919. (Gárate Córdoba)

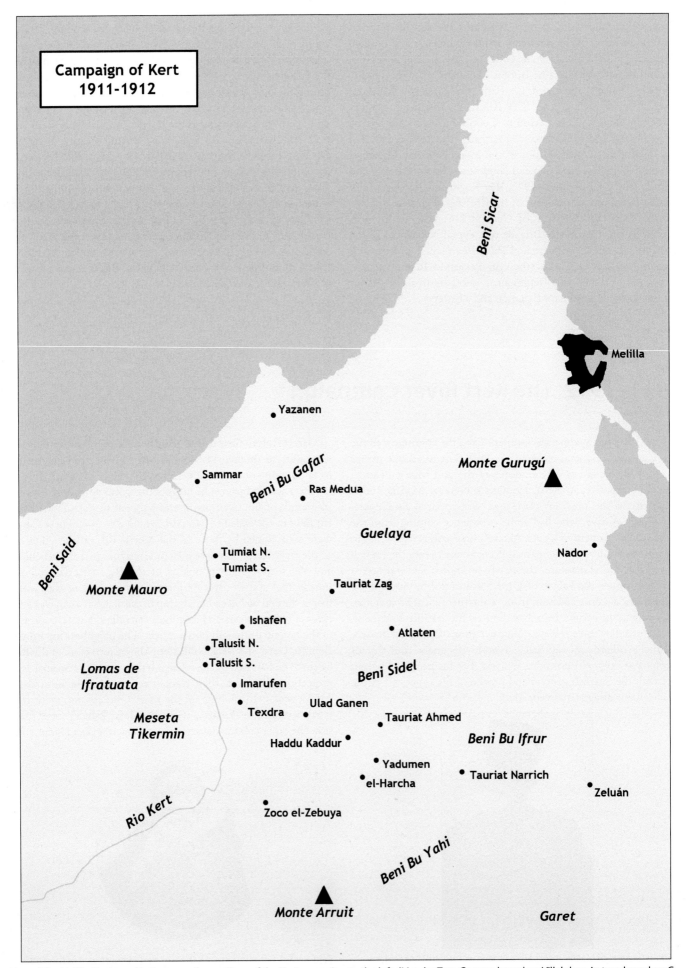

**Campaign of Kert
1911-1912**

Beni Sicar

Melilla

Yazanen

Beni Bu Gafar

Monte Gurugú ▲

Sammar

Ras Medua

Guelaya

Nador

Beni Said

Tumiat N.

Tumiat S.

▲ Monte Mauro

Tauriat Zag

Ishafen

Atlaten

Talusit N.

Talusit S.

Lomas de
Ifratuata

Imarufen

Beni Sidel

Texdra

Ulad Ganen

Meseta
Tikermin

Tauriat Ahmed

Haddu Kaddur

Beni Bu Ifrur

Yadumen

Tauriat Narrich

el-Harcha

Zeluán

Rio Kert

Zoco el-Zebuya

Beni Bu Yahi

▲
Monte Arruit

Garet

Map of the Melilla Region with the area of operations of the Kert campaign to the left. (Map by Tom Cooper, based on Villalobos, in turn based on C. Martínez de Campos, *España Bélica*)

A convoy moving along a zigzagging track to arrive to the Harcha position. (via Gárate Córdoba)

King Alfonso XIII, called "El Africano" (The African), reviewing Cazadores in Fuerte Camellos, Melilla in 1911. (Marín Ferrer)

the whole area for Spain almost without fighting, although the expeditioners had the support of the local Harkas that were grouped in Zoco el Hach: those of Beni Sicar, under Abd el Kader (a former rebel against Spain in 1909), Beni Bu Gafar, Buhe, and Beni Sidel, under a different pro-Spanish Mizzián. At the same time, on 20 June the government created the first regular forces made up of Rifian soldiers, who would be used as a shock force, as they knew the terrain and the population better. Incidentally it would improve the public image of the war, as the casualties would be more evenly distributed and fewer coffins would arrive in the ports of Spain. Thus, the *Fuerzas Regulares Indígenas* were created, a mixed force of infantry and cavalry of 900 Moroccan soldiers (including 99 horsemen) under Lieutenant Colonel Dámaso Berenguer, who would later form the 1st Tabor of Melilla.[2]

Fighting in the Kert

However, the situation of peaceful occupation soon ended: on 24 August, a group of engineers escorted by two companies of the África Regiment who were charting the terrain near Ishafen were forced to flee by the Rifians. They suffered four deaths, two of them being beheaded, their heads carried on stakes. The rebels consisted of about 500 warriors of Hach Amar from the kabyles of M'talsa, Beni Bu Yahi and Beni Said, all of them coming from across the river Kert, or south of it, at its source. On 29 August, General García Aldave sent a punitive column of 4,000 troops

of the Gourougou. They marched converging to the north, both columns arriving on 23 May 1911 at Ras Medua, a few kilometres from the Kert. The latter column was formed by a vanguard of the Indigenous Police under Lieutenant Colonel Salazar Saporta, followed by forces under Colonel Aizpuru, Lieutenant Colonel Vallejo Vidal, and further back, the reserve under General Orozco himself. They then occupied Tauriat Zag a month later, a little further south, Mount Harcha on 3 June, and on 1 August they moved near to the sources of the Kert. The advance subdued

under General Larrea, the 1st Half Brigade of the 2nd Mixed Cazadores Brigade, with allied kabyles from Beni Sidel, Mazuza, Beni Bu Gafar, Beni Bu Ifrur and Beni Sicar, under Abd el-Kader. These forces reoccupied Ishafen, guarding the middle course of the Kert, while the Harkas and the Cataluña Battalion crossed the river and plundered the neighbouring towns in reprisal. After a couple of days of raiding, the friendly Harkas returned to their territories. On 2 September, the Spanish left two guard posts on

A mounted artillery battery of 75mm Schneider cannons in Melilla. (Marín Ferrer)

General Larrea's column marching to the Kert in August 1911. (Gárate Córdoba)

Regulares troopers with an orphan Moor boy. (via Gárate Córdoba)

regiment of six batteries, half mounted, half mountain, and a regiment of engineers). As support units the Spanish had the 1st Half Brigade of the 2nd Mixed Cazadores Brigade, under General Gabriel Orozco Arascot, with the Cazadores battalions of Cataluña no. 1, Tarifa no. 5, and Ciudad Rodrigo no. 7 (4,200 soldiers), the Disciplinary Brigade (two companies), the cavalry Cazadores de Alcántara no. 14 Regiment (five squadrons), the artillery of the Melilla Command (seven batteries), a battery of the 7th Artillery Regiment, several support companies, the Regular Indigenous Forces of Melilla (320 soldiers) and the Indigenous Police of Melilla (500 soldiers). In total there were about 25,500 soldiers. These units were then reorganised into Ros Souza's 1st Brigade, Carrasco Navarro's 2nd Brigade and Orozco's 3rd Brigade.[3]

Both posts at Talusit were fired upon, and on the night of the 6th Hach Amar's Harka

the heights of North and South Talusit, opposite the Kert, and returned to their bases at Tauriat Zag.

At that time their forces in the Melilla Division under General Salvador Díaz Ordóñez were organised as follows: the 1st Brigade of General Joaquín Carrasco Navarro (regiments San Fernando no. 11, with 3,750 men, and Ceriñola no. 42 with 3,800 soldiers, and a machine gun group) and the 2nd Brigade of General Silverio Ros Souza (regiments Melilla no. 59 and África no. 68, each one with 4,200 soldiers, the new regiment of cavalry Cazadores Taxdirt no. 29 of five squadrons, a machine gun group, a mixed artillery

crossed the Kert, and a few hundred horsemen from M'talsa and Beni Bu Yahi attempted to take Imarufen, south of the Talusit, in the centre of the Spanish line. However, the mounted troops of the Taxdirt/ 2nd Brigade of the Melilla Division, and the Indigenous Police moved ahead and managed to occupy the town before the Rifians, supported by troops of the 1st Brigade (four Ceriñola and San Fernando companies) as well as a friendly Harka. To the south-east, General Orozco advanced with his 1st Half Brigade of Cazadores from Yadumen, enveloping the right of the Rifians when attacking Imarufen, and eventually defeating them. The Spaniards had 40 casualties, but Hach Amar lost half of his troops by this enveloping attack, returning to cross the river again.

Then, García Aldave ordered that garrisons were to be left in Imarufen and Ishafen, which dominated the north and south of the heights of Talusit respectively. Feeling secure, he ordered the Talusits to be abandoned, which the Rifians would not take long to reoccupy. Meanwhile the Spaniards continued reinforcing. On 9 September the 2nd Half

A machine gun section at the Kert. (via Gárate Córdoba)

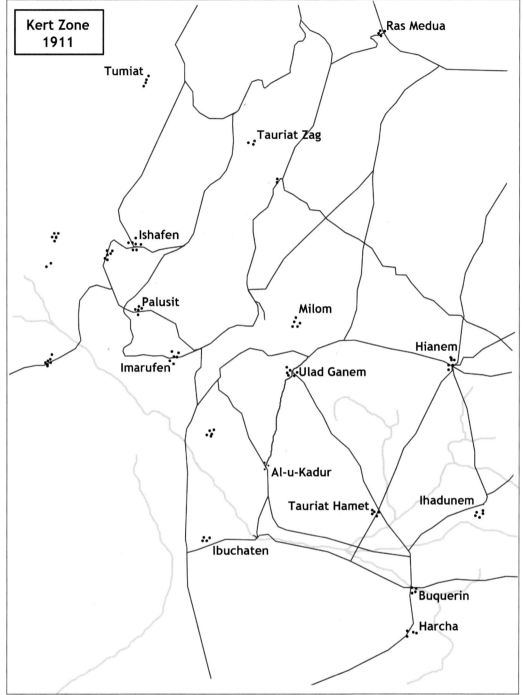

Map of the Kert area of operations in August and September 1911. (Map by Tom Cooper based on Gárate Córdoba)

Laureate. Colonel Astilleros, of the San Fernando Regiment, in the most advanced post of Ishafen, made another sortie to pursue them, but the Rifians turned back, ambushed him and finished him off. Even so, the Moors went back to the Kert at dawn. At Imarufen, further south, the troops of the Ciudad Rodrigo Battalion made another sortie, which dispersed the enemy. There, Captain Jiménez Ortoneda won the Laureate, as despite being shot in the chest continued to lead the attack until he was left on the battlefield. The combat must have been hard, as the Spaniards had 155 casualties.[4]

Meanwhile, García Aldave continued to accumulate troops, this time with the arrival of the 2nd Brigade of the 4th Organic Division, under General Francisco Villalón Fuentes, formed by the regiments Extremadura no. 15 (1,800 soldiers in two battalions), Borbón no. 17 (as No.15) and a machine gun group. Thus, the forces available in Melilla already amounted to 35,000 soldiers, grouped in the Melilla Division and the Expeditionary Forces (2nd Cazadores Half Brigade and 2nd Brigade/4th Division). However, before they could launch their offensive, Hach Amar's Rifians crossed the Kert again on the 20th, occupying the Talusit, the heights between Ishafen to the north and Imarufen to the south. Colonel Eugenio García Gómez departed with the Melilla Regiment from Imarufen and managed to recapture the Talusit at the cost of 77 casualties. Finally, at the end of September, new Spanish reinforcements arrived, this time the 1st Brigade of the 5th Organic Division, under General Juan Pereyra Morante, with the regiments Mallorca no. 13 and Guadalajara no. 20 (each with two battalions of 1,800 men), a machine gun group and three mountain batteries.

Thus, García Aldave now had 41,570 soldiers and finally decided to cross the Kert on 7 October: Colonel Primo de Rivera's column, with the *San Fernando* Regiment, would cross the Kert from Imarufen, to the south, to cover the flank of the main assault. Such would be the one of General Orozco's 1st Half Brigade of Cazadores, that would cross further south at Zoco el-Zebuya, to ravage the M'talsa camps, and then, turning north to reach the

Brigade of Cazadores (battalions Segorbe no. 12, Chiclana no. 17 and Talavera no. 18, about 2,700 soldiers) arrived. With the arrival of these troops the front was reorganised, and the 1st and 2nd Brigades of Ros y Carrasco's Melilla Division moved to Ishafen, where the divisional command post under Díaz Ordóñez was located, and the 1st Half Cazadores (also named as 3rd Brigade), went to Imarufen. However, the Rifians were also reinforced on the other side of the river, with contingents from the central Rif, from Bocoya and Beni Urriaguel, followed by warriors from Beni Said, Beni Tuzin, Beni Ulixek and Temsaman. On 12 September they crossed the Kert again, attacking Ishafen and Imarufen, but were held back by artillery and machine guns. A bayonet charge by a section of the África Regiment and another of the San Fernando Regiment, in Ishafen, dispersed them, winning 1st Lieutenant Carpintier Valverde and 2nd Lieutenant Martínez Cortes the

Table 3: Spanish Forces for the Kert Campaign (1911)		
Melilla Division (General Salvador Díaz Ordóñez)	1st Brigade (General Carrasco Navarro) (later, 2nd Brigade)	San Fernando no. 11 Regiment (3,750)
		Ceriñola no. 42 Regiment (3,800)
		Machine Gun Group
	2nd Brigade (General Silverio Ros Souza) (later, 1st Brigade)	Melilla no. 59 Regiment (4,200)
		África no. 68 Regiment (4,200)
	Support	Cazadores Taxdirt no. 29 Cavalry Regiment (5 squadrons)
		Machine Gun Group
		Mixed Artillery Regiment (6 batteries)
		Engineers Regiment
2nd Cazadores Brigade of Gibraltar (General Gabriel Orozco) (later, 3rd Brigade in operations)	1st Half Brigade (later 3rd Brigade, to the Melilla Division)	Cataluña no. 1, Tarifa no. 5, Ciudad Rodrigo no. 7 Cazadores battalions (4,200)
	2nd Half Brigade (since mid-September, to the Expeditionary Forces)	Segorbe no. 12, Chiclana no. 17, Talavera no. 18 Cazadores battalions (2,700)
Expeditionary Forces	2nd Brigade/4th Organic Division (General Francisco Villalón) (mid-September until end of November, returning again from December)	Extremadura no. 15 Regiment (1,800, two battalions)
		Borbón no. 17 Regiment (1,800, two battalions)
		Machine Gun Group
	1st Brigade/5th Organic Division (General Juan Pereyra Morante) (from October)	Mallorca no. 13 Regiment (1,800, two battalions)
		Guadalajara no. 20 Regiment (1,800, two battalions)
		Machine Gun Group
		Three mountain batteries
	Support	Disciplinary Brigade (two companies)
		Cazadores de Alcántara no. 14 Regiment (five squadrons)
		Melilla Artillery Command (seven batteries)
		7th Artillery Regiment (one battery)
		Regular Indigenous Forces of Melilla (320)
		Indigenous Police of Melilla (500)

Tikermin plateau, to turn east and cross the river again at Imarufen. General Orozco met stiff resistance in crossing the river, which had to be forced at the bayonet by the *Cataluña* Battalion, and then, after burning Tikermin, he returned as planned. Before Orozco's action, further north, the San Fernando Regiment crossed the river and took the hills of Ifratuata, at the foot of Monte Mauro, the main rebel base of the Beni Said. However, it was a hornet's nest, and after Orozco's departure, the Moroccans attacked the San Fernando, Colonel de Rivera being wounded and replaced by Colonel Tomasetti. On the verge of collapse, the regiment was supported by other elements of the Melilla Division who replaced it. On the 8th, the fire continued in Ifratuata as the Rifians were reinforced by the Beni Urriaguel and Temsaman. Tomasetti was finally able to retreat after suffering 117 casualties, as the Spaniards, to his rear, had retaken Talusit, leaving his route clear. The temporary occupation of Talusit was made by two columns

from the Division of Melilla that converged from the north, in Ishafen, and the south, in Imarufen. However, again abandoned, these heights were reoccupied on 14 October by the Moors. In this firefight, General Díaz Ordóñez was mortally wounded, being replaced by General Francisco Aguilera. In the end, this offensive had been too much for nothing: after gathering huge numbers of troops General García Aldave had limited himself to a punitive operation on the other side of the river Kert, and the rebellion was still as active as ever, ready to harass the kabyles loyal to Spain on the other side.[5]

The Great Offensive of El Mizzián
With the situation at a standstill, General García Aldave planned a landing in the Moorish rear, at the Bay of Alhucemas (Al Hoceima) in the central Rif, to attack the kabyles of Beni Urriaguel, Bocoya and Temsaman from behind. They would count on the support

A convoy made of trucks going to the Kert. (via Gárate Córdoba)

The Kert River valley showing the sector where the Rifians attacked (1); the Alcazaba (fortress) where they took shelter and that was bombed by the artillery (2); and the final position of the rebels (3). (via Gárate Córdoba)

of the river through which the Rifians were sneaking in to make their incursions. Thus, the Spanish line that protected the Kert, about 60km long, was formed by a series of posts from the sea, to the north, at Beni Bu Gafar, to the plains of the Garet, to the south, at Beni Bu Yahi and M'talsa. In the middle it had additional posts at Ishafen, the Talusit heights, Imarufen, and Texdra, and further to the south-east, at the Harcha, Yadumen and Tauriat Narrich. Apparently, the Rifians calmed down and asked for a truce, so on the 27th, General García Aldave repatriated the 2nd Brigade/4th Division to Spain, with the Borbón and Extremadura regiments.[6]

However, on 21 December, the Moors led by El Mizzián himself, violated the truce and crossed the Kert again, invading Beni Bu Gafar and Beni Sidel. This time Mizzián counted on numerous troops, since kabyle men arrived from French Morocco itself, coming from Fez and Taza. The Rifians would surround the Spanish front line positions to the north (Beni Bu Gafar) and south (Beni Sidel). Their right wing had to advance until they reached the southern slope of the Gourougou, reconquer their kabyle of Beni Bu Ifrur, and raise the whole Guelaya in arms again. Thus, this southern flank slipped north of Ishafen and reached the Spanish

of a person settled in Axdir, Beni Urriaguel, called Abd el-Krim el Khattabi, the father of the famous Abd el-Krim, who paradoxically in a few years would become a headache for Spain. Abd el-Krim's contacts with Spain were discovered and his house was burnt down by the Rifians, so he had to seek refuge in Melilla itself. With the disembarkation ruled out, General García Aldave returned to focus on the Kert front and on 16 November he definitively occupied the heights of Talusit, closing the gap in the central part

Soldiers taking care of an injured soldier in the Kert. Note the Ros caps. (Gárate Córdoba)

General Salvador Díaz Ordóñez, commander of the Melilla Division, who died in October 1911 on the Talusit heights. (Gárate Córdoba)

rear, attacking Tauriat Zag on 23–24 December. To do so, they occupied a height overlooking the position, and from there they assaulted it from two different points, reaching the barbed wire fences with the Rifians even throwing stones and the crosses of a nearby cemetery, and setting fire to a fodder depot. General García Aldave then sent five columns to assault the heights occupied by the Moors in front of Tauriat Zag, Lieutenant Colonel Bernáldez being killed together with 20 men. The following day another nine Spaniards fell, together with many wounded. Seeing that it was impossible to dislodge them, General García Aldave decided to clear the flanks of the Rifians, so on 27 December he launched an attack against the northern or left flank of El Mizzián. There were five columns under General Aguilera with troops of the 1st Half Brigade of Cazadores and the 2nd Brigade. They set out making a semicircle from Yazanen (north-east, near the coast), Zoco el-Had, Ras Medua and Avanzamiento (inland, further east) and then approached the river again, from Ishafen, to clear all of Beni Bu Gafar kabyle, pushing northwards, until they reached the mouth of the river, supported by a flotilla of gunboats. The columns of Carrasco Navarro, Aizpuru and Regoyos came from the east, and those of Ros and Serra from the south. With his northern flank enveloped, El Mizzián abandoned the attack on Tauriat and retreated to the north-west, to Sammar, almost at the mouth of the river. There, seeing himself surrounded and with his back against the Kert, he decided to break the Spanish line by attacking the southern column, which was coming up precisely along the riverbank. There, he fell against General Ros's column, with troops of the 2nd Brigade of Melilla. Ros was wounded, and Colonel García Gómez, who replaced him, fell dead. Despite the support of the naval fire and the arrival of the other columns, El Mizzián crossed the Kert, and took refuge in Mount Mauro, in Beni Sidel, after perhaps losing about 500 warriors in the combat. For its part, Spain achieved this victory at the cost of some 397 casualties.[7]

Clearing the Southern Flank and the Garet

General García Aldave, seeing how hard the fighting was and how the attack on the northern flank had worked, changed his strategy for a more aggressive but indirect one, ready to envelop the Kert's sources from the south. To this end, he requested new reinforcements: two battalions and two companies from the Serrallo Regiment arrived from Ceuta; the 2nd Brigade/4th Division (Bourbon and Extremadura regiments) or Villalón Brigade, returned from Malaga, as the Wad Ras and Saboya regiments; six cavalry squadrons (from the Lusitania, Alfonso XII and Villarrobledo regiments); and three batteries. The troops were then reorganised: General Aguilera's Organic Division was created (the San Fernando, Ceriñola, África and Serrallo regiments, four squadrons

of the Taxdirt Regiment, and four mountain batteries); General Larrea's Provisional Division (Extremadura, Borbón, Saboya and Wad Ras regiments, four squadrons of the Alcántara Regiment, five batteries); the 2nd Mixed Brigade of Cazadores; and a whole Cavalry Brigade, foreseeing operations in the Garet Plain. They would also have a Group of Machine Guns, a battery, two Harkas of friendly Moors, a battalion of Indigenous Police (six Mías of the Harkas of Quebdana, Beni Sicar, Beni Bu Ifrur, Beni Bu Gafar and Beni Sidel, adding up to 663 soldiers), and six Tabors and three squadrons of the Regulares. General Francisco Gómez Jordana would act as Chief of Staff of García Aldave in place of General Larrea, who now assumed command of one of the divisions.[8]

On 18 January 1912 General Larrea invaded the hostile kabyle of Beni Bu Yahi, to the south, still on the east bank of the Kert,

Troops of the Regiment Saboya in Nador, that also fought in the 1911–1912 campaign. (via Gárate Córdoba)

Generals Valeriano Weyler, Minister of War (in white, the man who nearly won the war in Cuba), Gómez Jordana and Fridich in Ishafen. (via Gárate Córdoba)

Table 4: Melilla Forces in the Kert (1912)

Organic Division (General Francisco Aguilera)		San Fernando, Ceriñola, África, Serrallo regiments
		Taxdirt Regiment (four squadrons)
		Four mountain batteries
Provisional Division (General Larrea)		Extremadura, Borbón, Saboya, Wad Ras regiments
		Four squadrons of the Alcántara Regiment
		Five batteries
Reserve	2nd Mixed Brigade of Cazadores	Cataluña, Tarifa, Ciudad Rodrigo, Segorbe, Chiclana, Talavera Cazadores battalions
	Cavalry Brigade	Lusitania, Alfonso XII, Villarrobledo regiments
	Group of Machine Guns	
	A battery	
	Two Harkas	
	Battalion of Indigenous Police	
	Indigenous Regulares (six Tabors, three squadrons)	

with a column of Regulares (now consisting of six companies and three cavalry squadrons), and four columns of his Provisional Division and Cavalry Brigade, some 20,000 troops. As the Rifians faced this avalanche of men in a plain with no mountains in which to take refuge, they did not put up a fight, and after suffering only 56 casualties the Spaniards occupied Monte Arruit, and then returned to the north. In Monte Arruit they left General Villalón's 2nd Brigade (Extremadura and Borbón regiments) as a garrison.

Meanwhile, El Mizzián, seeing the Kert front unguarded by this massive displacement of troops, crossed the river again, occupying the Tumiat heights, north of Ishafen, in Beni Bu Gafar, and threatening the mouth of the river. Also, in the centre, the area between Texdra and Harcha, or further south, by Zoco el-Zebuya, remained open to crossing. General García Aldave then prepared the operations to close these gaps definitively. From 19 to 22 February a young 18-year-old 2nd Lieutenant called Francisco Franco, in the África Regiment, received his baptism of fire in the area of Imeyaten, Tifasor and Sammar. On 22 March, at the mouth of the river, the Tumiat and Sammar heights were recovered with naval support, taking advantage of

Captain Llanderas's artillery battery at Ishafen on 22 March. (via Gárate Córdoba)

General Carrasco Navarro's camp in Yadumen, the water of which was contaminated with oil on 11 March 1912. (Gárate Córdoba)

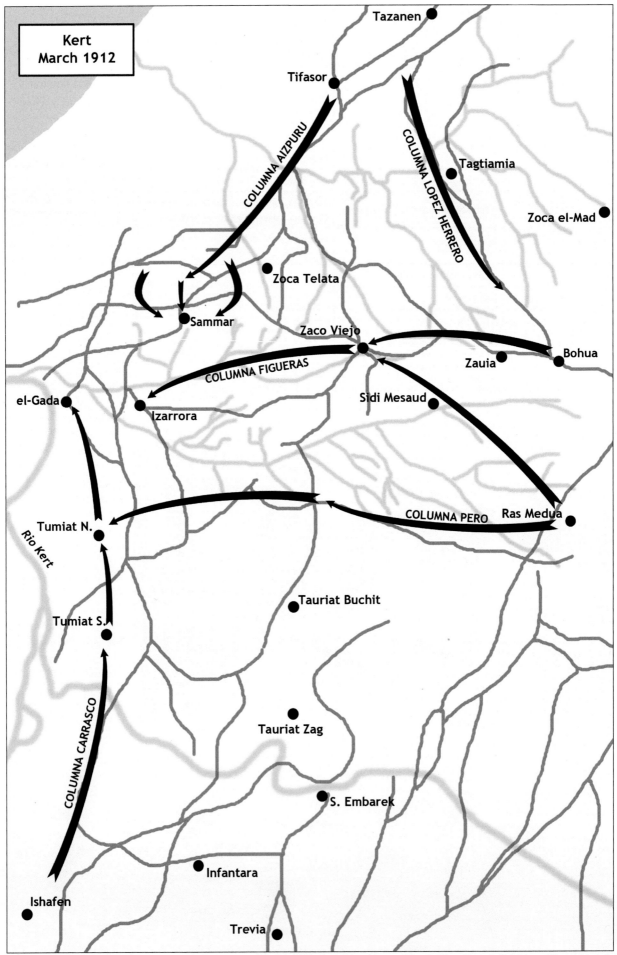

Kert
March 1912

Tazanen

Tifasor

COLUMNA AIZPURU

COLUMNA LOPEZ HERRERO

Tagtiamia

Zoca el-Mad

Zoca Telata

Sammar

Zaco Viejo

Bohua

COLUMNA FIGUERAS

Zauia

el-Gada

Izarrora

Sidi Mesaud

Tumiat N.

COLUMNA PERO

Ras Medua

Rio Kert

Tauriat Buchit

Tumiat S.

Tauriat Zag

COLUMNA CARRASCO

S. Embarek

Infantara

Ishafen

Trevia

The area of operations of the Kert in March 1912, with the movements of the Spanish columns. (Map by Tom Cooper based on Gárate Córdoba)

This Rifian warrior is shown wearing traditional clothing and carries a captured Spanish Mauser 7.65mmx53mm rifle. The Rifians were mainly armed with the 1893 or 1916 model Spanish Mausers, bought, captured or smuggled into Morocco, or old hunting weapons or single shot Remington 11mm rifles. The Indigenous Police would also have had a similar appearance when on campaign, though they wore uniforms in their barracks. (Artwork by Anderson Subtil)

This trooper of the Spanish Legion wears a turned-down collar jacket with a typical light green shirt, typical of the Legion, just visible, breeches with green leggings, Valencian espadrilles, and an English Mills belt acquired in Gibraltar. On his head, he wears a *chambergo* or large stitched canvas hat, more appropriate than the typical tasselled Elizabethan cap, to give protection from the sun. (Artwork by Anderson Subtil)

This native Moroccan trooper is a member of the Regulares, the best troops of Spanish Army until the appearance of the Legion. He wears a red *tarbuch*, the typical hat of the Regulares (somewhat similar to the well-known Fez), a chickpea-coloured jacket, and a blue sash, which indicates that he was a member of the 2nd Group of Regulares of Tetuán (originally coming from Melilla). He carries the severed head of a Rifian rebel, since according to some unconfirmed reports, the Larache Command paid a bounty for them. According to legend, one Regular trooper asked for more money for the head of his own father. (Artwork by Anderson Subtil)

This figure shows a Lieutenant of the Cazadores of Lusitania cavalry regiment, as he would have appeared in 1909. A squadron of this unit fought at Taxdirt but did not participate in the famous charge. He wears the "*rayadillo*" uniform typical of 1909-1914, consisting of white with a narrow blue stripe, and a Wolseley salacot (sun helmet). He is armed with a Spanish-made Orbea nº 7 revolver, a copy of the American Smith & Wesson No. 3 Double Action. Note the skull and crossbones badge of the regiment on the collar; this was won in the battle of Madonna del Olmo, in 1744, Italy, earning the regiment the name 'the Hussars of Death'. (Artwork by Anderson Subtil)

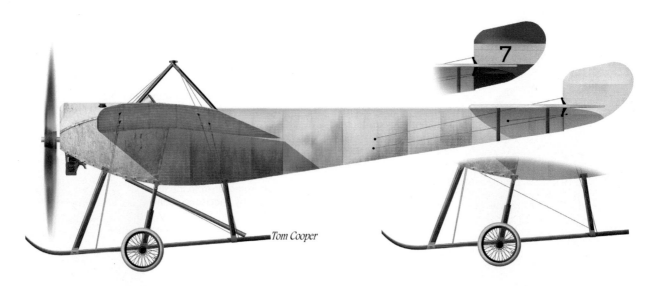

At least four Nieuport IVG/VIMs were deployed to Tetuán in 1913, being then moved to Zeluán, Melilla, in 1914. This sample made the first crossing of the Gibraltar Strait, flown by captains Herrera and Ortiz Echagüe, on 14 Feb 1914, hence probably the first flight linking two continents. They wore no markings initially, but during the First World War, the Spanish flag was applied on the fin. Specifications: 120 km/h; power to weight ratio 0.08 (37.5 Kw engine, 490 Kg loaded weight); ceiling 2,500m. (Artwork by Tom Cooper)

Four Austrian-made Lohner Pfeilfliegers were deployed to Tetuán in 1913, conducting the first reconnaissance flight of the Spanish aviation. They were also used by captains Barrón and Cifuentes on 17 Dec 1913 for the first ever attack made using an optical device to aim bombs. All were originally painted in silver-dope overall and wore no markings or insignia: the Spanish flag was applied on the ruder during the First World War. Specifications: 130 km/h; power to weight ratio 0.08 (67.5Kw engine, 879Kg loaded weight); ceiling 2,700m; range 300KM. (Artwork by Tom Cooper)

Developed in Spain as an improved version of the Lohner, the Barrón W – designed by Captain Barrón – were manufactured in 1917. Up to six were sent to Tetuán in May 1919 but retired before the end of the year. This type was specifically designed to use the excellent Spanish Hispano-Suiza V8 engine and had the wing shape amended to improve the visibility of the observer. Specifications: 150 km/h; power to weight ratio 0.09 (105Kw engine, 1,150 Kg loaded weight); ceiling 4,750m. (Artwork by Tom Cooper)

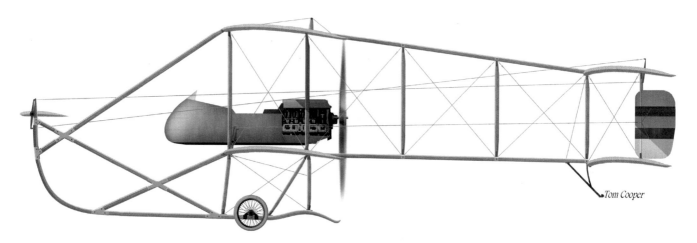

Four Maurice Farman MF.7s were deployed at Tetuán in October 1913, being operational until the end of 1919, but being progressively replaced by the MF-11s and Barróns. They earned the nickname of "Longhorn" due to the superstructure in the nose resembling horns or antennas. This plane was the first to be attacked by Rifians, with the crew of two injured and earning the first Laureate of the Spanish aviation. Specifications: 95 Kms/h; power to weight ratio 0.06 (52kw engine, 855 Kg loaded weight); ceiling 4,000m; range 300KM. (Artwork by Tom Cooper)

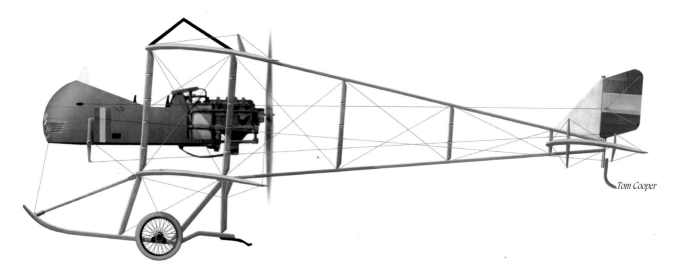

Replacing worn-out MF.7s, at least six Maurice Farman MF.11s were deployed at Arcila in 1915. These aircraft were operational until June 1917. In Spain, both the MF-7s and 11s were known as of "Aceitunas" (Olives) due to their olive green paint and the shape of the cockpit, which held two crew. Note the aviation insignia on the nose. Specifications: 117 Kms/h; power to weight ratio 0.08 (75kw engine, 930 Kg loaded weight); ceiling 3,800m; range 400KM. (Artwork by Tom Cooper)

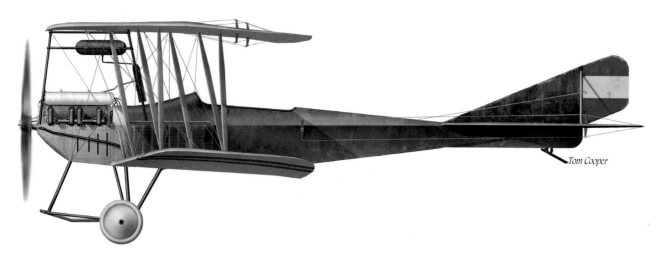

Developed in Spain through a significant re-design of the Lohner Pfeilflieger, Barrón Flechas – designed by Captain Barrón – were manufactured in 1915 and 1916. Starting from 1917, up to 18 were deployed to Spanish Morocco to replace worn-out MF.11s, Lohners, and Nieuports. About 12 of them had the excellent Spanish Hispano-Suiza 8A engine, the first ever with a water-cooled V8 cylinder disposition and one of the best engines of the First World War (some 48,000 of 250Kw the 8F variant were built). Specifications: 160 km/h; power to weight ratio 0.1 (105Kw engine, 1,000 Kg loaded weight); ceiling 4,750m. (Artwork by Tom Cooper)

The Spanish RIF WAR

Despite most narrations stating that the Rif War began in 1920, shortly before the Disaster of Annual, in reality it ignited in 1909. This map shows the main area of the operations vs El Mizzian, in Melilla-Gurugu (1909) and the river Kert (1911-12); vs El Raisuni (1911-1920); and finally the offensive and defeat of Silvestre in Annual, vs Abd el Krim. The war would end in 1927. (Map by Anderson Subtil)

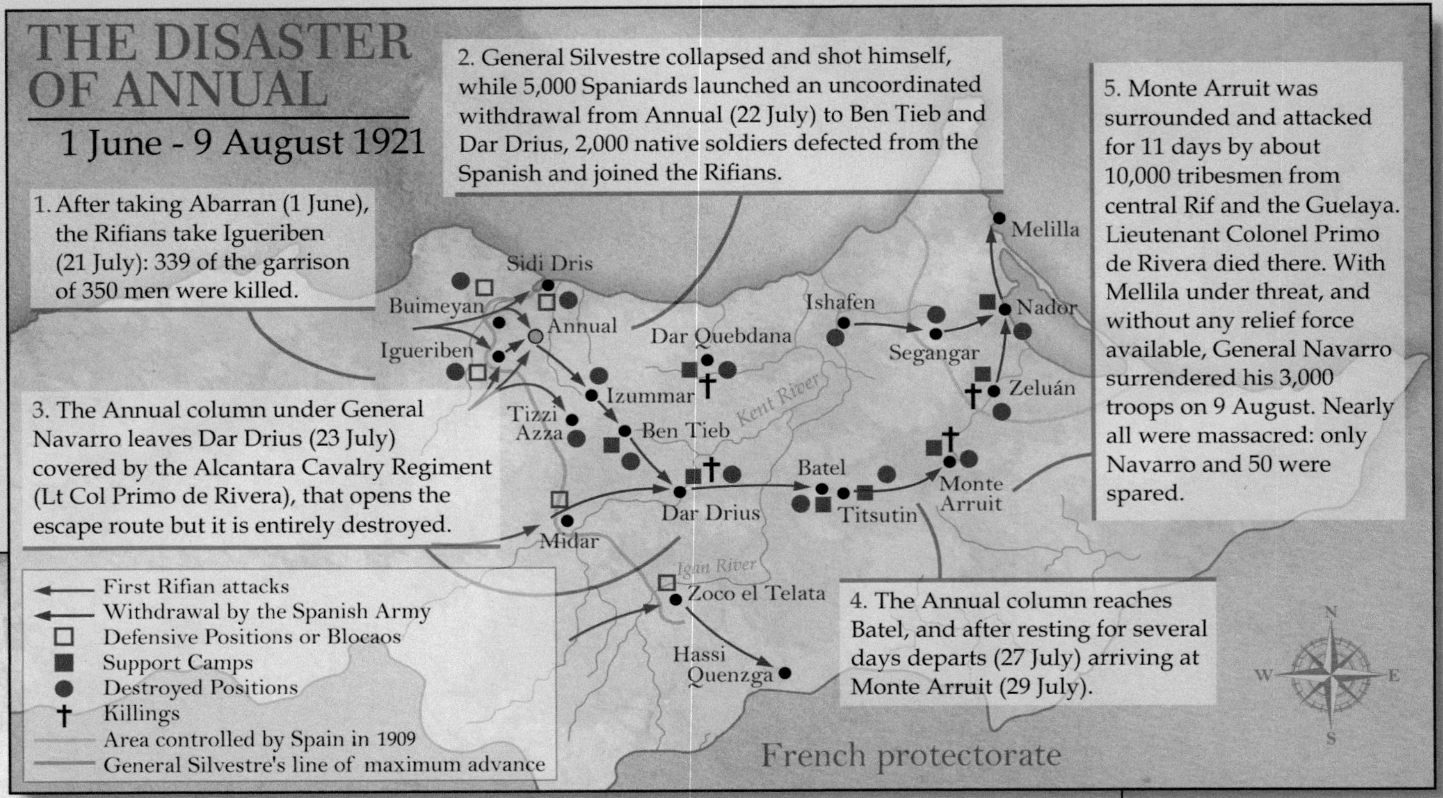

THE DISASTER OF ANNUAL
1 June - 9 August 1921
1. After taking Abarran (1 June), the Rifians take Igueriben (21 July): 339 of the garrison of 350 men were killed.
2. General Silvestre collapsed and shot himself, while 5,000 Spaniards launched an uncoordinated withdrawal from Annual (22 July) to Ben Tieb and Dar Drius, 2,000 native soldiers defected from the Spanish and joined the Rifians.
3. The Annual column under General Navarro leaves Dar Drius (23 July) covered by the Alcantara Cavalry Regiment (Lt Col Primo de Rivera), that opens the escape route but it is entirely destroyed.
4. The Annual column reaches Batel, and after resting for several days departs (27 July) arriving at Monte Arruit (29 July).
5. Monte Arruit was surrounded and attacked for 11 days by about 10,000 tribesmen from central Rif and the Guelaya. Lieutenant Colonel Primo de Rivera died there. With Mellila under threat, and without any relief force available, General Navarro surrendered his 3,000 troops on 9 August. Nearly all were massacred: only Navarro and 50 were spared.
First Rifian attacks
Withdrawal by the Spanish Army
Defensive Positions or Blocaos
Support Camps
Destroyed Positions
Killings
Area controlled by Spain in 1909
General Silvestre's line of maximum advance
Sidi Dris
Buimeyan
Annual
Igueriben
Dar Quebdana
Izummar
Tizzi Azza
Ben Tieb
Kent River
Dar Drius
Midar
Igan River
Zoco el Telata
Hassi Quenzga
Batel
Titsutin
Monte Arruit
Ishafen
Segangar
Nador
Zeluán
Melilla
French protectorate
N
W
E
S

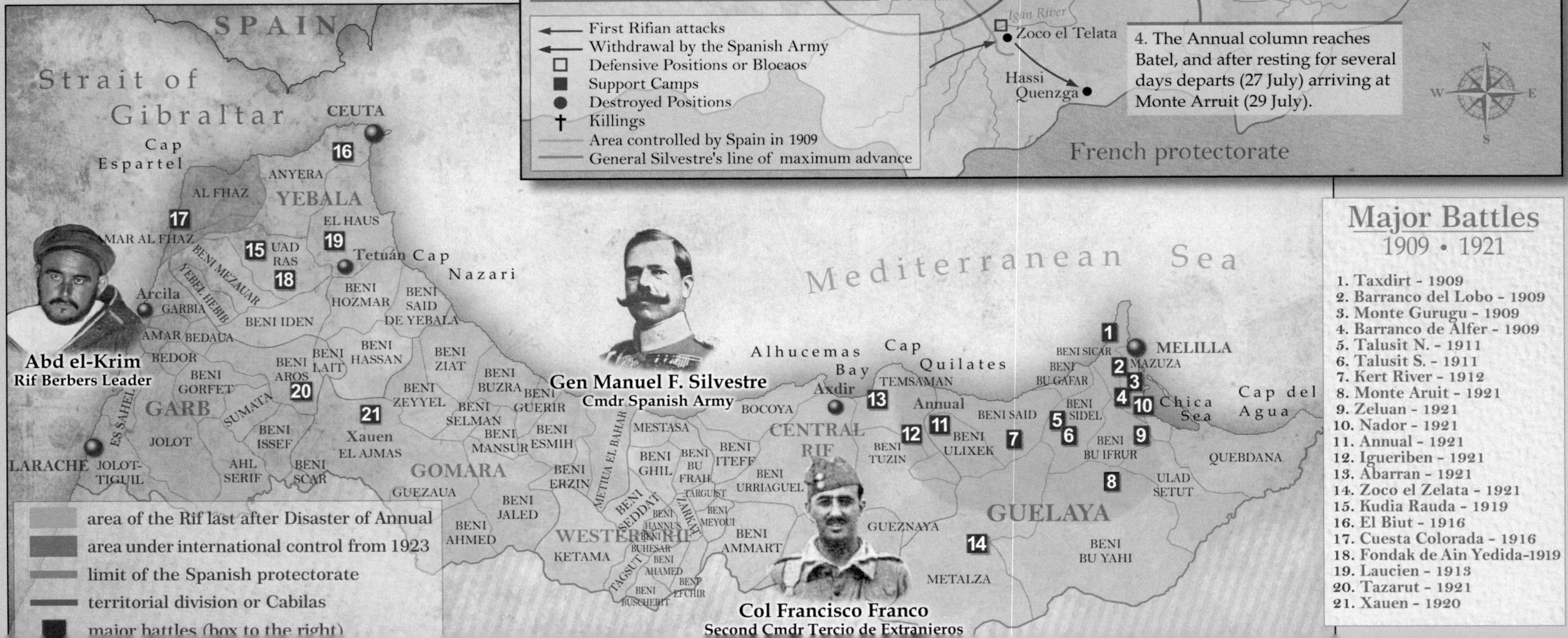

SPAIN
Strait of Gibraltar
CEUTA
Cap Espartel
ANYERA
AL FHAZ
YEBALA
EL HAUS
Tetuán
Cap Nazari
MAR AL FHAZ
BENI MEZAUAR
YEBEL HEBIB
UAD RAS
Arcila
GARBIA
BENI IDEN
BENI HOZMAR
BENI SAID DE YEBALA
AMAR BEDAUA
BEDOR
BENI GORFET
GARB
SUMATA
BENI AROS
BENI LAIT
BENI HASSAN
BENI ZIAT
Mediterranean Sea
Abd el-Krim
Rif Berbers Leader
Gen Manuel F. Silvestre
Cmdr Spanish Army
Col Francisco Franco
Second Cmdr Tercio de Extranieros
LARACHE
ES SAHEL
JOLOT
JOLOT-TIGUIL
AHL SERIF
BENI ISSEF
BENI SCAR
Xauen
EL AJMAS
GOMARA
GUEZAUA
BENI ZEYYEL
BENI BUZRA
BENI SELMAN
BENI MANSUR
BENI GUERIR
BENI ESMIH
BENI JALED
BENI AHMED
WESTERN RIF
KETAMA
BENI ERZIN
METIUA EL BAHAR
MESTASA
BENI GHIL
BENI BU FRAH
BENI ITEFF
BENI URRIAGUEL
BENI AMMART
TARGUIST
ZARKAT
BENI MEYOUI
BENI SEDDAT
BENI HANNUS
BUHESAR
AHAMED
BENI EFCHIR
BENI BUSCHERIT
TAGSUT
Alhucemas Bay
Axdir
BOCOYA
CENTRAL RIF
Cap Quilates
TEMSAMAN
Annual
BENI TUZIN
BENI ULIXEK
BENI SAID
GUEZNAYA
METALZA
GUELAYA
BENI SICAR
BENI BU GAFAR
BENI SIDEL
BENI BU IFRUR
MELILLA
MAZUZA
Chica Sea
Cap del Agua
QUEBDANA
ULAD SETUT
BENI BU YAHI
area of the Rif last after Disaster of Annual
area under international control from 1923
limit of the Spanish protectorate
territorial division or Cabilas
major battles (box to the right)
Major Battles
1909 • 1921
1. Taxdirt - 1909
2. Barranco del Lobo - 1909
3. Monte Gurugu - 1909
4. Barranco de Alfer - 1909
5. Talusit N. - 1911
6. Talusit S. - 1911
7. Kert River - 1912
8. Monte Arutt - 1921
9. Zeluan - 1921
10. Nador - 1921
11. Annual - 1921
12. Igueriben - 1921
13. Abarran - 1921
14. Zoco el Zelata - 1921
15. Kudia Rauda - 1919
16. El Biut - 1916
17. Cuesta Colorada - 1916
18. Fondak de Ain Yedida-1919
19. Laucien - 1913
20. Tazarut - 1921
21. Xauen - 1920

the fact that at that moment the bulk of the Rifians were on the southern flank. The Aizpuru column marched from the north, at Tifasor, to occupy Sammar. López Herrero's column, further back, went down to the south and then turned west to occupy Izarrora, converging there with the Figueras and Perol columns, which, coming from Ras Medua, had taken Tumiat before. Finally, the Carrasco column, from the south, in Ishafen, also covered the Tumiat. Meanwhile, further south, El Mizzián had infiltrated again to the rear, in the Spanish defensive flank, and they attacked the column of General Carrasco Navarro (battalions of Chiclana, Ciudad Rodrigo, Talavera, two companies of Cataluña, two squadrons of Taxdirt and two batteries, totalling 3,477 soldiers and 562 horses). Carrasco Navarro had left Yadumen (or Ihadumen), to explore the gap between Texdra and Harcha. The Spaniard fulfilled his reconnaissance mission, and on his return a cavalry charge made by the Taxdirt squadrons drove the Rifians out of Ulad Ganen, but as he continued the march and left Tauriat Ahmed, the Moors rushed in, occupied the town and began shooting at General Carrasco Navarro's rearguard (the Cataluña and Ciudad Rodrigo battalions). There, Captain Accame launched

a bayonet charge that drove the Moors out. Accame was shot twice, once in the belly, and died just as the battle ended, earning the Laureate. The Spanish suffered 138 casualties, including Chiclana's Lieutenant Colonel Gómez de Avellaneda.[9]

The government, overwhelmed, ordered the suspension of operations, but El Mizzián continued his own: on 11 May he crossed the Kert again from the south, at Zoco el-Zebuya, and turning north again threatened the Spanish rear at Tauriat Ahmed. Carrasco Navarro's Brigade, which was still there from its previous withdrawal, went out to attack him, being repulsed by Mizzián's fire. Subsequently, El Mizzián was detected to the north-east, at Ulad Ganen, perhaps trying to envelop the whole Spanish line from behind, and again General Carrasco Navarro attacked him on the 13th. The Spanish again suffered heavily with 119 casualties.

However, the general would soon get his revenge. With El Mizzián advancing between Spanish positions, General García Aldave improvised an offensive with 14,250 men and 1,100 horses (15 battalions, 12 squadrons, seven batteries, and four companies of Regulares and four of sappers) in concentric columns to trap

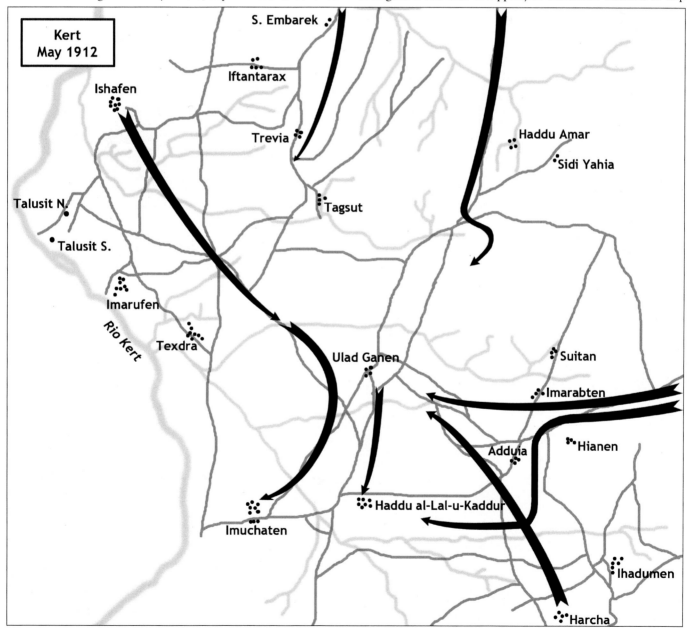

Map of the Kert River area of operations in May 1912, with the Spanish columns move, that led to the death of El Mizzián. (Map by Tom Cooper based on Gárate Córdoba)

General Carrasco Navarro after taking Kaddur, in the campaign that led to the death of El Mizzián. (Gárate Córdoba)

Captain Accame (centre) and his assistant Manuel Chaves (to the left of Accame), who died leading a counterattack in Tauriat Ahmed, winning the Laureate. The third soldier remains unidentified. (via Gárate Córdoba)

2nd Lieutenant Francisco Franco of the África Infantry Regiment, had his baptism of fire in February 1912, in Sammar, the Kert, being also present in the action that led in March to the death of El Mizzián. This picture was dedicated to his father: "Love and hugs, Paco (Francisco)". (via Gárate Córdoba)

him. First, he would close his routes of march creating positions in a triangle formed by Ulad Gannen, to the north, Haddu Kadur, to the south-east, and Tauriat Ahmed to the east. Six columns departed towards these points: the Moltó column, from the north-west, next to the Kert, in Ishafen, which would converge towards the south-east, to Ulad Gannen, and then would continue further south, to Imuchaten. The columns Villalba and Figueras, would go from Ras Medua, towards Tagsut, north to south direction. The Rodríguez and López Herrero columns would

Lieutenant Samaniego, of the Melilla Regulares, in the centre, who was shot dead in his last charge to kill El Mizzián. (via Gárate Córdoba)

also converge from the east, in Avanzamiento, towards Ulad Ganen. And finally, General Carrasco Navarro, with up to 2,200 soldiers, was to go from Harcha, in the south, to the north-west, converging on Ulad Ganen, and then turning south and taking Haddu Kadur. Among Carrasco Navarro's troops were two young lieutenants who within a decade would become famous: Francisco Franco and Emilio Mola. Carrasco Navarro left at dawn on the 15th. His vanguard consisted of three squadrons of Melilla Regulares on the left, and two squadrons of Taxdirt on the right, under Lieutenant Colonel Berenguer. On

Regulares cavalry charging, such as those led by Lieutenant Samaniego that killed El Mizzián. (via Gárate Córdoba)

The Regulares squadron deployed, with the section of Lieutenant Samaniego on the right. (via Gárate Córdoba)

Policía Indígena and friendly Harkas identifying the corpse of El Mizzián. (via Gárate Córdoba)

Sergeant Kaid Hassani Mohammed and Corporal Gonzalo Sauco, from the Regulares de Melilla, who killed El Mizzián. (Gárate Córdoba)

at the cavalry of the Regulares, and their leader, wrapped in a robe, began to shout for them to defect. Lieutenant Samaniego, of the Regulares cavalry, charged at him with his horse, and was hit with a shot in the belly, but in agony or perhaps inertia, the Lieutenant continued his charge until he reached the Rifian leader, who had to fire six shots from his revolver into the horse to stop him. However, a Moroccan sergeant of the Regulares and a Spanish corporal took the opportunity to shoot the Rifian leader, who fell dead next to the body of Lieutenant Samaniego. It was none other than El Mizzián. Among his clothes they found a rosary and a Koran. For this action Lieutenant Samaniego was awarded the Laureate, posthumously.

Carrasco Navarro had finally taken revenge and, at the cost of 92 casualties, had just won the war for Spain, albeit somewhat fortuitously. After the fall of the legendary leader, the kabyles began to dissolve. In July those of Beni Bu Yahi and Beni Said surrendered, as did El Mizzián's personal Harka, now under the command of Sidi Baracca. Hach Amar tried to reinforce his kabyle of M'talsa without success, and finally surrendered. At last, and after suffering 2,400 casualties (500 dead), Spain had carried her lines solidly to the Kert River and pacified the whole of Guelaya. Spain began the withdrawal of troops, returning the Serrallo Regiment and the Machine Gun Group to Ceuta, and the rest to Spain, so that by the end of the year only the 2nd Cazadores Brigade and the 2nd Brigade of the 1st Division, some 10,000 men, remained in Melilla. In any case, with the eastern sector pacified, Madrid would not cross the Kert again until eight years later, in 1920, shortly before the Disaster of Annual.[10]

leaving their camp at Yadumen they were supported by an infantry battalion, crossing a stream which was under fire from the Rifians. Suddenly, a group of 25 horsemen came out of a ravine and fired

4

1911–1921: Ceuta, the War in the West

While all these episodes took place in the eastern part of Morocco, in the western part the fighting was always more intermittent and less bloody. In general, the Anyera kabyle, which surrounds Ceuta, was hostile to the Spanish, except for the faction closest to them, those of Beni Mesauar, which in fact cooperated with General García Aldave, who in 1909 was in command of the Ceuta region. This faction asked Spain for protection because El Raisuni was trying to annex the whole of Anyera. El Raisuni was the leader of a bandit gang, later converted into a Mehala of the Makhzen, and was flexible and cunning, combining cooperation with the Sultan and Spain with pure confrontation. Sick with dropsy to the point of deformity, he had little in common with Sean Connery, the actor who made him famous in the film *The Wind and the Lion*.

However, he was a somewhat novelistic and poetic character: he escaped from prison in 1898, and in 1904 he became famous for kidnapping westerners, which forced President Roosevelt to send a fleet to Tangier. In the meantime, El Raisuni distracted his victims, among them the millionaire Perdicaris, with excursions to the Yebala and banquets, allowing them also to send chronicles to the press about their stay. El Raisuni, as rebel against the Sultan, defeated his forces in 1908, and forced his appointment as Bajah (Bajá) of Arcila and governor of the Yebala. In his first indirect actions against Spain, an attempt to build a road linking Ceuta to Tetouan was in fact blocked by him, fearing an expansion of Spanish influence in the area. The new commander of Ceuta, General Felipe Alfau, decided to ignore the threats of El Raisuni

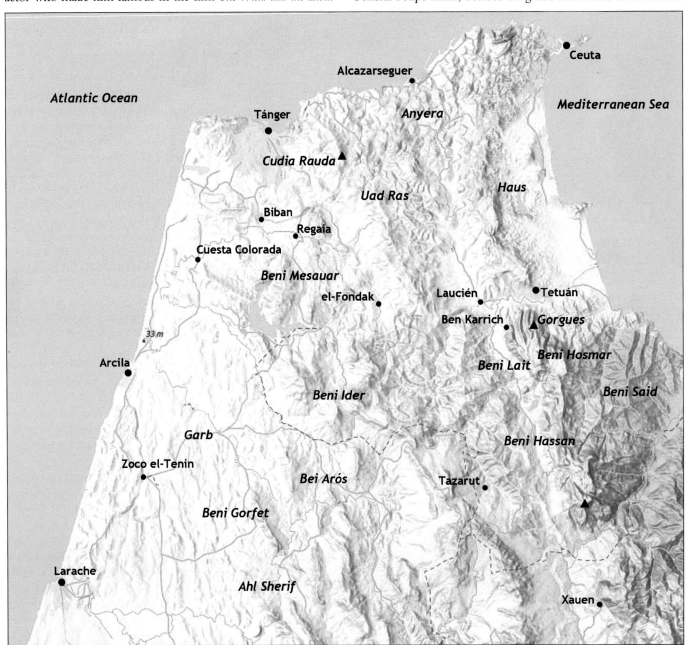

Map of the Ceuta region area of operations, with Tangier (Tánger), Arcila and Larache to the left, and Xaouen (Xaúen) and Tetouan (Tetuán) to the right. (Map by Tom Cooper, based on Villalobos)

Cuartel del Rey, Ceuta. These barracks would be the first base of the newly created Spanish Legion in 1920. (via Carrasco García & de Mesa)

Ahmed al Raisuli, also known as El Raisuni, was the leader of a group of bandits in Yebala. He became the Bajá of Arcila, sometimes collaborating with the Spaniards, sometimes fighting against them. He ended his days as a prisoner under Abd el-Krim. The attractive figure of Sean Connery, who played him in the film *The Wind and the Lion* has nothing in common with him, as he was ill with dropsy. His words about his enemy, General Silvestre, were famous and prophetic: 'You and I form the storm; you are the furious wind; I am the calm sea … I, like the sea, never leave my place, and you, like the wind, never stay in yours'. Silvestre would die in Annual precisely for advancing too far. (via Gárate Córdoba)

and began to expand the perimeter of Ceuta by occupying Cudia Federico, Cudia Afersian, Cudia Fajama and Altos de la Condesa with Regulares on 7 March 1911. Then Monte Negrón and La Restinga on the 22nd, and in the month of May he moved to a mere 11km north of Tetouan, at Rincón de Medik. This was done without fighting and in preparation for the occupation of Tetouan, in accordance with the negotiations that were being carried out to define the Spanish Protectorate in Morocco, which was closed in November 1912. Thus, on 19 February 1913, General Serrano entered Tetouan by surprise but without a fight, from Medik (south of the El Haus kabyle), with a force of two battalions, a squadron and forces of Regulares and Rif sharpshooters. Thus, the north-eastern area of the Yebala came under Spanish rule.

In the meantime, as already noted, due to the terrible impression caused by the arrival of hundreds of Spanish corpses in the Peninsula (which had led to the Tragic Week in Barcelona in 1909, and numerous anarchist terrorist attacks), Madrid continued with its policy of creating native Moroccan forces as shock troops. Thus, between 1910 and 1912, four Tabors of Indigenous Police were created in the western zone (Tangier, Tetouan, Larache and Casablanca, despite being in the French area).[1]

The *Panther* Incident

At the same time, in the extreme south-west of the Protectorate, on 8 June 1911 Spain occupied Larache on

The Larache Policía Indígena, formed mainly by recruits from sub-Saharan Africa, wearing parade dress. (via Carrasco García & de Mesa)

Larache Policía Indígena, seen in June 1911, that later would be transformed in the Regulares of Larache. (via Carrasco García & de Mesa)

Two views of Larache: the Zoco (market) to the left, the beach to the right. (via Gárate Córdoba)

Officers of the 1st Marine Infantry Battalion, which occupied Larache in 1911. (via Gárate Córdoba)

A cavalry patrol crosses the Lucus River in the Larache Sector. (via Gárate Córdoba)

Lieutenant Colonel Fernández Silvestre departing for operations. The aggressive Silvestre was promoted beyond his capabilities, being one of the main factors leading to the Disaster of Annual in 1921. (via Gárate Córdoba)

the Atlantic coast, in the area known as the Garb, Lucus, Arcila or Utauien, (Holot Tiguil kabyle), by disembarking three marine companies and 50 sailors from the cruiser *Cataluña*. The next day, a company of marines and two sections of the Larache Tabor advanced inland following the Lucus River, towards the Jolot kabyle, to then take Alcazarquivir on 10 June. With this advance Spain closed the way to any French attempt to occupy the area from the south. In fact, the occupation was a preventive measure since at the same time France had taken Fez on 20 May to create its Protectorate and was getting dangerously close to the Spanish zone. There, Lieutenant Colonel Manuel Fernández Silvestre, of Annual's sad memory, was appointed commander of the area. He received the 4th Company of the Marine Expeditionary Battalion, another marine battalion, and three squadrons of the

Vitoria Regiment. Lieutenant Colonel Silvestre had two problems to solve. The first one was the Khalifian Mehala of the Sultan of Morocco, which with French instructors was being formed near Alcazarquivir and, on the other hand, the private Mehala, based in Arcila, of El Raisuni. This bandit had called Spain to his aid to get rid of the French presence, but he did not want Madrid to hinder his actions either. Following the advice of El Raisuni, decorated by Spain, Lieutenant Colonel Silvestre occupied Zoco el-Tenin in the south, which controlled the Garb area, and, to the north, the coastal town of Arcila itself. From there, he marched east taking Akba el-Hamara or Cuesta Colorada, which controlled the road leading to Tangier, even further north, in order to communicate between the two areas of Spanish presence in the west. With these actions Lieutenant Colonel Silvestre was also expelling the French Mehala that was in the area, though in a peaceful way.

Meanwhile, the French and Spanish unilateral occupations angered Germany, which also wanted its slice of the African cake, so on 1 July it sent the gunboat *Panther* to Agadir to press for land, but this scheme failed due to the refusal of the United

Colonel Silvestre and the Bajá of Alcazarquivir lead the march to occupy Cuesta Colorada. (via Gárate Córdoba)

Kingdom. Nevertheless, France was given a free hand in Morocco by Germany on 4 November, and Spain was forced to sign a new Spanish-French agreement on 14 November 1912, by which Spain ceded to France 70,000 square kilometres of the Moroccan Protectorate, to compensate for what France had ceded in the Congo to Germany.[2]

The Double Game of El Raisuni

In 1912 Silvestre was promoted to colonel and his forces increased to three marine infantry battalions, two line infantry battalions, two groups of machine guns, two Tabors of Regulares, several police Mías and a naval company. However, the problems with El Raisuni soon began. The kabyle of Ahl Sherif, east of Alcazarquivir complained about the exactions practised by El Raisuni, so Colonel Silvestre occupied Arcila, in the north, the capital of the bandits, on 17 August 1912, and demanded that he dissolve his Mehala. El Raisuni proposed that he do so gradually, so as not to lose prestige among his followers, but Silvestre took it as a delay and ended up assaulting his base in Ulad Bu Maisa, on the 30th, suffering 4 casualties. El Raisuni's words to the irate Colonel Silvestre would be prophetic when the Disaster of Annual took place years later:

> You and I form the storm; you are the furious wind; I am the calm sea. You arrive and blow irritably; I shake, I stir, I burst into foam. The storm is already there. But there is a difference between you and me: I, like the sea, never leave my place, and you, like the wind, never stay in yours.

The Rifian fled to Tangier, and in January 1913 he began to organise the insurrection: in Muley Abd es-Selam, the kabyles of Ajmas, Beni Aros, Beni Hassan, Beni Hosmar, Beni Ider, Wad Ras, Haus and Anyera proclaimed Mohammed Ould el-Taguezarti as Sultan of Yebala, and gathered a Harka in Ben Karrich, south of Tetouan, in the kabyle of Beni Hosmar. The Raisuni, double-dealing, warned General Alfau that a rebellion was being prepared. As a first reaction, on 19 February Alfau occupied the city of Tetouan, south of Ceuta, in El Haus, without a

fight, as already seen, and in June he moved the Melilla Regulares Group to the west, and reinforced Larache, in the Garb. Also, the Indigenous Police was organised, which on 24 April had four Tabors, named Alcazarquivir, Tetouan, Larache and Arcila, with 254 soldiers each.

On 5 June a separate group of Rifians, perhaps following instructions from El Raisuni, attacked the position of Cudia Fraicatz, on the road to Larache, Zoco el-Tenin and Zoco el-Telata, and further west (Beni Gorfet kabyle). Colonel Silvestre sent two columns on the 18th in retaliation, but Beni Gorfet's forces now moved further south, attacking Minzah, near Alcazarquivir (Jolot kabyle), and against the city of Alcazarquivir again on 7 July. They were repulsed at the foot of the wall by Commander Queipo de Llano (an outstanding figure in the 1936 civil war), with the cavalry of the Group of Larache Regulares. On 11 August, Colonel Silvestre himself led a punitive expedition occupying Cuesta Colorada, to

Larache Policía Indígena in 1913. (via Carrasco García & de Mesa)

A view of the Cuesta Colorada from Tetouan, occupied by Colonel Silvestre, with a Regulares rider in the foreground. (via Gárate Córdoba)

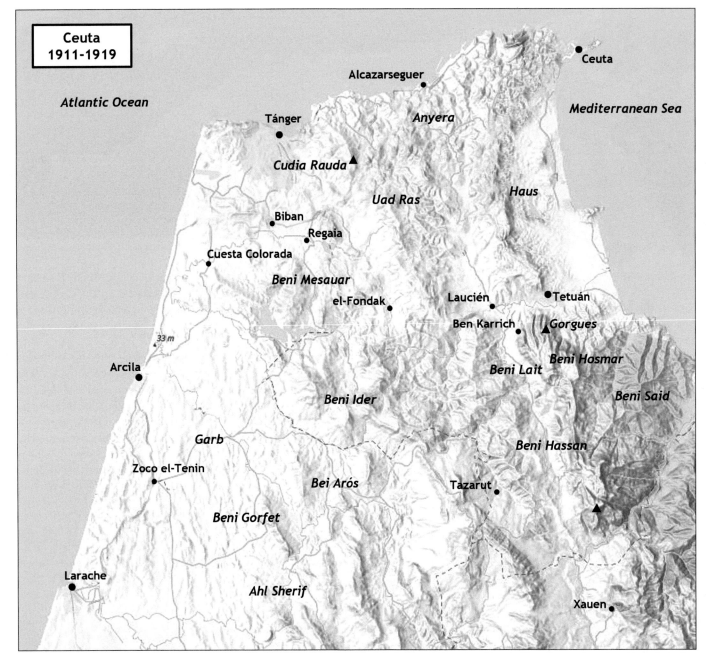

Ceuta 1911-1919

Atlantic Ocean

Mediterranean Sea

Ceuta

Alcazarseguer

Tánger

Anyera

Haus

Cudia Rauda ▲

Uad Ras

Biban

Regaia

Cuesta Colorada

Beni Mesauar

Laucién ● Tetuán

el-Fondak

Ben Karrich ▲ Gorgues

33 m

Beni Hosmar

Arcila

Beni Lait

Beni Said

Beni Ider

Garb

Beni Hassan

Zoco el-Tenin

Bei Arós

Tazarut ▲

Beni Gorfet

Larache

Ahl Sherif

Xauen ●

Map of the area of operations against El Raisuni, in 1911–1919, in between Tanger, Arcila and Larache. (Map by Tom Cooper, based on Marín Ferrer)

the north, between Arcila and Tangier. His idea was to contain El Raisuni, who had been operating from his base in Zinat since May. Then, Colonel Silvestre carried out several campaigns to clear all the plains of the Garb and expel the rebels to the mountainous areas, for which he would be promoted to general. With such a rapid rise, nobody had the time to discover how aggressive but emotionally unstable a man General Silvestre was.[3]

The Defensive Lines of Tetouan-Ceuta and Larache

A little further east, the rebellion in the area south of Tetouan under Ould el-Taguezarti seemed more dangerous because of the large number of kabyles that joined him. On 11 June, the General Commander of Ceuta, General Larrea, ordered General Primo de Rivera's brigade of Cazadores to occupy Laucién, 5km from Tetouan, a wedge between Wad Ras and Beni Ider kabyles. After leaving a garrison there and returning to the city, the Spaniards were attacked, and in the confusion the Arapiles Battalion fired on their comrades. In the following actions on the lines of communication of this position, the Spaniards suffered

hundreds of casualties. In just the occupation operation and the following day the losses amounted to 211 men. Young Lieutenant Franco, who had asked to be transferred to the shock units of the Regulares, would intervene from 21 June, and it is here where Franco began to create his fame: General Berenguer himself asked who commanded a section that was advancing particularly well: "Franquito" (due to his short stature) was the answer. Around the same time, a bullet tore the coffee thermos out of Franco's hands, but he was unharmed, so that his Moroccan soldiers began to say that he had *baraka* (in Arabic) or "luck". Despite the constant attacks, Laucién was held. The Spanish counteroffensive began from this position: first against Beni Ider and the Harka established at Ben Karrich, south-west of Tetouan, and then to the north, on the lines of communication with Ceuta, at Yebel Dersa and the Mountains of Haus kabyle. By now the Spanish columns began to make punitive expeditions rather than occupy new territory, but the new strategy seemed to be working, dissuading the kabyles from acting due to having to protect their own villages.

General Berenguer, wearing a Regulares uniform, giving instructions to his Regulares. (via Gárate Córdoba)

Burning buildings near Laucién. (via Gárate Córdoba)

Captain Franco with Commander Serrano with the new Regulares. Franco, as with other valiant and ambitious officers, asked to be moved to the Regulares, the best unit in the Spanish Army at the time and always in the forward posts. Here the legend of "Franquito" (little Franco), and his "baraka" (luck) was born. (via Gárate Córdoba)

Commander General of Larache Manuel Fernández Silvestre. (via Gárate Córdoba)

However, in August General Alfau resigned as High Commissioner because of his friction with the commander of Ceuta, and was replaced by Lieutenant General José Marina, the same man who had led the pacification of Melilla in 1909. Lieutenant General Marina went to Ceuta to repel the attacks against the city itself. The Spanish troops were organised into two sectors: one under General Menacho, in Ceuta, which would act to clear the so-called Anyera gap to the west, and another under General Aguilera, in Laucién, next to Tetouan. On 7 September, in General Menacho's area, the Anyera kabyles were dispersed when Colonel Francisco Arráiz de la Conderera made a sortie against the Biutz to clear the positions of Cudia Federico, Cudia Afersian and Cudia Fajama. Although Colonel Arráiz did not manage to reach the Biutz because of enemy fire, the Moors suffered much damage and left the area. The so-called Anyera gap was closed at the cost of suffering only 25 casualties. To the south, in Tetouan, on 22 September, there was fighting at Izarduy, where the young Lieutenant Franco, in command of a Melilla Regulares section, stood out again by rescuing several wounded on the 27th. Throughout October and November new positions were established to defend friendly villages, and in December a Moorish offensive against Laucién, west of Tetouan, was aborted

when the Spaniards struck further north, at the Hayera River, at the village of El Haus, and at Loma Amarilla.

By the end of the year, the Spanish had created a fortified line of 102 positions defended by 22,000 troops between Ceuta (Anyera), El Rincón (south, at El Haus), Tetouan, and the Martín River. In the south-western area of Larache, General Silvestre did the same by creating a fortified line with 14,000 soldiers from the French border north to the international zone of Tangier. The deployment of these units was as follows: in the Tetouan area there were 12 battalions of line infantry (from the Regiments Inmemorial del Rey (1st Battalion), Mallorca, León (1st Battalion), Borbón, Saboya (1st Battalion), Ceuta, Wad Ras and Córdoba); four Cazadores battalions of the 1st Brigade (Madrid, Barbastro, Arapiles and Llerena); the cavalry of the Vitoria Regiment (four squadrons) and that of Regulares (three squadrons); a machine gun group; a Tabor of Regulares; nine artillery batteries; and four companies of sappers. In the Rincón area there were two battalions, two companies, and a machine gun group, a section of the 1st Squadron of the Vitoria Regiment, and a battery of the 1st Mountain Regiment; and in the Ceuta area, there were 12 line infantry battalions (Ceuta, Serrallo, Estella and

Command	Sector	Regiment/Brigade	Battalion or Subunit
Ceuta	Tetuán	Inmemorial del Rey	1st Battalion
		Mallorca	1st–3rd Battalions
		León	1st Battalion
		Borbón	Elements
		Saboya	1st Battalion
		Ceuta	Elements
		Wad Ras	1st–3rd Battalions
		Córdoba	1st–3rd Battalions
		1st Brigade Cazadores	Madrid, Barbastro, Arapiles, Llerena
		Vitoria (Cavalry)	Four squadrons
		Regulares (Cavalry)	1st–3rd Squadrons
		Machine Gun Group	
		Regulares	One Tabor
		Artillery	Nine batteries
		Sappers	Four companies
	El Rincón		Two battalions
			Two companies
		Machine Gun Group	
		Vitoria (Cavalry)	Section/1st Squadron
		1st Mountain Artillery	One battery
	Ceuta	Ceuta	1st–3rd Battalions
		Serrallo	1st–3rd Battalions
		Estella	1st–3rd Battalions
		Borbón	1st–3rd Battalions
		Two Machine Gun Groups	
		Albuera (Cavalry)	One squadron
		Villarrobledo (Cavalry)	One squadron
		Vitoria (Cavalry)	One squadron
		Artillery Group	Eight batteries
		Engineers	Two companies
Total at Ceuta			22,000 soldiers
Larache	Larache	Extremadura	1st Battalion
		Reina	1st Battalion
		Expeditionary Marine Infantry	1st–3rd Battalions
	Arcila	Covadonga	1st–3rd Battalions
		Guadalajara	1st–3rd Battalions
	Other	Cazadores	Figueras, Las Navas
Total at Larache			14,000 soldiers

Table 5: Forces Deployed in the Tetuán-Ceuta and Larache Defensive Lines (1914–1915)

Navas. Artillery, engineer and native troops of the Regulares and Indigenous Police should be added at these deployments in Ceuta and Larache. Outside the defended zone were the rebel Harkas, the main one being that of El Raisuni, with its troops in Zinat.[4]

The Birth of Spanish Military Aviation

Spanish Military Aviation was born on 7 March 1911, and after some hesitant beginnings it was finally considered ready to be used in war. This was a very advanced step, since the only precedents were the Italian experience in Libya, the Balkan War and the Mexican Revolution, before the Great War turned the military use of aeroplanes into something routine. Thus, the Minister of War ordered the formation of a squadron with aircraft from Cuatro Vientos, Madrid, on 18 October 1913, and authorised the use of Sania Ramel, Tetuán, as an aerodrome. The 1st Expeditionary Squadron would be commanded by Captain Alfredo Kindelán Duany (future commander of the rebel air forces in 1936, and later of the Spanish air forces), and would be formed by pilots captains Eduardo Barrón (who had acquired the Lohner planes in Vienna) and Alfonso Bayo; and the lieutenants Royal Prince Alfonso de Orleáns y Borbón, Jenaro Olivé, Julio Ríos Angüeso, Antonio Espín, Luis Moreno Abella, Carlos Alonso Llera and Carlos Cortijo (also the doctor of the unit). The squadron had 11 aircraft: three Nieuport VI-M monoplanes, four Maurice Farman MF-7 biplanes known as "Longhorns" because of the long front scaffolding that resembled antlers, and four Austrian Lohner Pfeilflieger biplanes. In Spain they also received the nickname "*Aceituna*" (olive), due to the green olive paint and the shape of the cabin. On the 23rd the planes, disassembled, were transported by ship, and once landed, were assembled by the pilots themselves. Lieutenant Alonso Llera, in a Nieuport, made the first flight from Tetuán on 2 November, which lasted eight minutes. Shortly afterwards, Alfonso de Borbón and Kindelán took off in a

Borbón Regiments), two machine gun groups, four squadrons of the Vitoria, Albuera and Villarrobledo Cavalry Regiments, an artillery group and eight batteries, and two engineer companies. The forces of the Larache Command were, in Larache city, the Extremadura (one battalion) and Reina (one Battalion), and the Expeditionary Marine Infantry Regiments; and in Arcila, further north, the Covadonga and Guadalajara Regiments. Also, the Larache Command had two Cazadores battalions, Figueras and Las

Table 6: The Expeditionary Squadrons		
Captain Alfredo Kindelán Duany		
Sania Ramel (Tetuán Aerodrome)		
Type	**Number of aircraft**	**Notes**
Nieuport VI-M	Three (later four)	Departed to Selouane, Melilla, to form the 2nd Squadron, being replaced in June 1917 by the Barrón Flechas
MF-7 Longhorns	Four	Three moved to Arcila, then to Larache, being replaced progressively since 1915 by the MF-11s
Lohner Pfeilflieger	Four	Being replaced in June 1917 by the Barrón Flechas
Morane Saulnier G	Three	Arrived in December 1914 to Tetuán, being replaced in June 1917 by the Barrón Flechas

According to some sources this was the first flight of the Spanish military aviation in Africa, in a Nieuport VI-M monoplane by Lieutenant Alonso Llera on 2 November 1913. (via Sánchez & Kindelán)

Spanish Royal Prince Alfonso de Orleáns y Borbón, an air enthusiast trained in France, who made the first Spanish reconnaissance flight in Africa and later would lead the Fokker Group in Alhucemas in 1925. (Orleáns-Borbón files, via Yusta Viñas)

Lohner to carry out the first reconnaissance mission over enemy territory. Soon, these planes were reinforced with three Morane Saulnier G Monoplanes. The first two samples were bought by the Count of Artal, as a present for the Spanish Army, and the third one by their own government. The first was piloted by Captain Ortiz Echagüe, taking off from Paris on 13 October, but he had to land in Bordeaux due to a fire in the engine that nearly destroyed the plane. The remnants of the machine and the two others were then carried by land and sea, arriving at Tetuán at the end of December. Then, Ortiz Echagüe rebuilt the destroyed plane and a new flight of three Moranes was briefly available in Africa. Once these planes passed to the reserve as trainers at Madrid, in 1917,

Lieutenant Martínez de Aragón made one of the first loops of the Spanish aviation.[5]

On 19 November, Kindelán ordered a reconnaissance of the area of Mount Cónico and Laucién by Farman MF-7 plate number 1 piloted by Lieutenant Ríos Angüeso and Captain Barreiro Álvarez as observer. Due to the thick vegetation on the mountain and the low clouds, Lieutenant Ríos Angüeso descended to fly at ground level, and Captain Barreiro made a sketch of the Rifian positions. However, just as he was about to finish, the Rifians shot Captain Barreiro in the chest and Lieutenant Ríos Angüeso in the belly and between the legs. Despite this, both crewmen helped each other as best they could and managed to return to Tetuán with the aircraft intact, surviving and being both decorated with the Laureate. These were the first casualties in combat for Spanish military aviation. With combat also in the Luccus area, to the south-west of the Protectorate, a second airfield was opened in Arcila under the

A pair of Henry Farmans in 1911, ready to depart from Cuatro Vientos, Madrid. More advanced planes, the Maurice Farman MF-7s, were deployed in Africa in 1913, but this view of the Henry Farmans gives us evidence of the fuselage and tail shape of the early MFs. (Ilustración Española y Americana, via Yusta Viñas)

Alfredo Kindelán, first pilot of the first graduating class, future commander of the aviation in Africa, and of the rebel forces during the civil war in 1936, controlling a Henry Farman in 1911. The MFs sent to Africa were similar, but with a closed and therefore more comfortable area for the pilot. (Archivo Histórico Ejèrcito del Aire, via Yusta Viñas)

Lieutenant Ortiz Echagüe (inset), and the Morane Saulnier acquired with funds from the Count of Artal (note the name "Artal" on the aircraft). (Nuevo Mundo, via Yusta Viñas)

Captain Eduardo Barrón, who arranged the acquisition of air bombs from Austria-Hungary and made the first bombing with a projectile specifically designed for aeroplanes and using aiming scopes. Also, he was the inventor of the Spanish Acedo and Barrón Flecha aeroplanes. (Heraldo Deportivo, via Yusta Viñas)

control of the Larache Command. Three Farmans departed from Tetuán with three pilots and three observers. Meanwhile, thanks to Barrón's efforts in Vienna, the first aviation bombs arrived. On 17 December, Captains Barrón and Carlos Cifuentes dropped four German Carbonit bombs on Ben Karrich from a Lohner. This was the first bombing in the world using bombs specifically designed to be dropped from an aeroplane with rudimentary aiming scopes (previously the bombs had been dropped by hand and by eye). In 1914, Captain Emilio Herrera took the command of the 1st Squadron in Tetuán, Kindelán being the head of aviation in Morocco.[6]

1914: The Regulares and Sanjurjo

In 1914, a sort of tacit agreement was reached, and operations slowed down, limited to firefights and isolated actions. The Spanish had secured their rear but did not continue to advance, and the Moors would not cross the Spanish lines to expand the rebellion. In the meantime, Spain took the opportunity to reinforce their Moroccan contingents. The idea was to create four types of indigenous units: the Mehalas of the Majzén, the Groups of Regulares, the Indigenous Police and the friendly Harkas, all of them formed by Moroccan recruits and NCOs, but led by Spanish volunteer

A detailed view of the cockpit and horns of a Maurice Farman MF-7 Longhorn, with the pilot Kindelán, chatting. (Orleáns-Borbón file, via Yusta Viñas)

A Lohner being prepared for the Royal Prince of Orleáns-Borbón. (Orleáns-Borbón file, via Yusta Viñas)

Pilots Kindelán, Vives, Infante and Abella, in front of a Lohner with its typical bat wings, in 1913. (Orleáns-Borbón file, via Yusta Viñas)

A detailed view of Barrón and Cifuentes in the cockpit of a Lohner. (Heraldo Deportivo, via Sánchez & Kindelán)

chiefs and officers. Being assigned to shock units, many officers (such as Lieutenant Franco) sought to be assigned to one of these units to improve their career prospects, even though they knew that their life expectancy was shorter – the Moroccans, although very brave, were only led by example, so the commanding officer had to always be at the front in all attacks to gain their trust. Moroccan names were used to designate these units: the Mehalas would be the European Regiments, the Tabors the battalions, and the Mías the companies. Thus, on 4 April, the Mía of the Jalifian Mehala of Tetuán was created. In July, two Mías were created in the Indigenous Police of Ceuta and three in that of Larache (named Larache, Alcazarquivir and Arcila, with the Tabors disappearing from that name). The most relevant units above all were the four Groups of Regulares of two infantry and one cavalry Tabor each (three companies and three squadrons each), organised by Emilio Berenguer Fusté. These units counted among their first commanders Commander Sanjurjo and Captain Mola, later prominent leaders in the civil war. These Groups were the 1st, from Tetuán (which originally came from Melilla); the 2nd, also recruited in areas of Melilla; the 3rd from Ceuta, formed with troops from Tetuán, from the Police of this area; and the 4th from Larache, from the Police Tabors of Larache, Alcazarquivir and Arcila. In January 1915, the 6th Mía of the Jalifian Mehala of Tetuán was created, and between this year and 1916, all the Indigenous Police battalions were increased to six Mías each. In December 1915, two cavalry Mías were created for the Jalifian Mehala of Tetuán, and every six infantry Mías ended up being grouped into two Tabors, and the cavalry into another, of 330 infantrymen and 150 horsemen in each. In 1917, three more Mías of the Indigenous

A view of two Farman Longhorns and a Lohner in Cuatro Vientos, Madrid, in September 1913. (Orleáns-Borbón file, via Yusta Viñas)

Lieutenant Colonel Federico Berenguer (brother of Dámaso, the founder of the Regulares), in conversation with the Moor Dris, in Arcila. (via Gárate Córdoba)

Police of Larache were created and in 1919 the friendly Harkas of Metugui (100 warriors) and Guelagui (50 men) were formed in the same district. In September 1919, the 9th Mía of the Larache Police was created. In November the Frontier Mía was created for Tangier, the 4th Mía of Ceuta merged with the 5th and 6th of Larache, so they formed six Mías in total in Ceuta, and another six in Larache. In 1920, two more Mías were created in Larache, and finally in 1921 the 15th Mía of Xauén was formed, adding up to a total of 30 Mías in the whole of the Spanish Morocco.[7]

In any case, the calm did not sit well with the rebels, who began their first internal fighting when, in January 1914, El Raisuni defied Taguezarti by proclaiming himself Sultan of Yebala in the capital of the rebels, the holy city of Xauén (El Ajmas kabyle), far south of Tetuán, in the area where the Gomara region begins. Many kabyle distrusted El Raisuni, so the rebellion lost momentum. In the meantime, El Raisuni continued with his double game and held conversations with Lieutenant General Marina. The few notable actions were the battle of Beni Salem, in an area between Tetuán and Malalien on 1 February. With Malalien defended by the Córdoba Regiment, a group made a sortie to clear the area and occupy Beni Salem (El Haus), 10km north of Tetuán, under General Aguilera. It was formed by two columns, in turn commanded by General Torres (with Peninsular troops) and General Berenguer (all formed by the new Regulares). To reach

Beni Salem, Berenguer had to cross a gorge, ordering Lieutenant Colonel Marzo to send Commander Sanjurjo with an advance guard, accompanied by Captain Emilio Mola. Sanjurjo managed to cross the gorge slowly, alone on horseback, while his soldiers were still on the ground, receiving a bullet in the hip and another that broke his arm. This brave feat of arms won Sanjurjo (the victor of the Rif War some 12 years later) his first Laureate. Franco was again one of the lieutenants in the action, who would later be promoted to captain the following year for the merits he had earned in this action. He would also be the youngest captain of the whole army, at the age of 22. Thus, in the same action and in the same unit the three main leaders of the military rebellion of 1936 are seen: Sanjurjo, Mola and Franco. Once the area was occupied, it came under the surveillance of the 2nd Battalion of the Inmemorial del Rey Regiment no. 1, in Primo de Rivera's column.

Afterwards, the actions were limited to shooting, examples including; the attack suffered by the Córdoba Regiment in the Negrón river on 3 April; or by the columns of General Santa Coloma in the Martín River on 4 May, which caused a retaliatory action on the Biutz the following day by Menacho and Arráiz's columns that hit into the void. In the Tetuán area, shootings were experienced in the Izarduy redoubt by the Cazadores de Arapiles, later relieved by the 1st Battalion of the Mallorca Regiment throughout June. In August these troops were relieved by the 2nd Battalion of the Inmemorial del Rey Regiment, and Primo de Rivera's brigade. Columns under Torres and Martínez Anido launched a punitive expedition from 20 to 22 June. On 28 June the convoy that was going from Cudia Federico (Anyera kabyle), escorted by horsemen from Cazadores de Estella, was heavily attacked, and had to be saved by Arráiz's column.

Meanwhile, in the west, General Silvestre expanded his lines to reach the border of the Tangier International Zone (a hotbed of arms smuggling), and to join his forces with those of Tetuán, to the west. Silvestre marched against El Fondak de Ain Jedida, in the south-east of Wad Ras. On 11 January Silvestre ravaged the Aicha River (Bedaua and Mezora), south of Arcila. Then, he returned to the south, to the area of Alcazarquivir, and on 13 January and 3 February he marched to punish the rebels of Ahal Serif. On the 16th, Silvestre himself departed with three columns (under lieutenant colonels Naveira, Berenguer and Saborido, the latter subdivided into two groups under commanders Nauvilas and Alonso), from Tzenin de Sidi el-Iamani, occupying Mount Mulai Buselhám, in the Sahel area, the Regiment of Las Navas suffering 20 casualties. Silvestre left Rafait on 11 May with the columns of lieutenant colonels León and Berenguer to close the accesses to the Beni Aros kabyle, to the east, and a third column converged towards them from Tzenin, under Commander Pérez de Lema, protecting the left flank and penetrating 7km. Throughout July, the Las Navas and Extremadura regiments were fired on in the Gaiton, General Silvestre reacting on 2 August with three columns (under Colonel Perales, Lieutenant Colonel Miranda and Commander Viana), which left Alcazarquivir to occupy Cudia Nebach and the Gaiton. At the same time, three other columns (under lieutenant colonels García Trejo, León and Colonel Navarro) left Larache and Arcila, to the west, supporting them and fixing the enemy. With these operations, the area could be cleared to build the Spanish-French railway from Tangier to Fez.

However, the outbreak of the Great War in August further limited operations, as Spain focused on guaranteeing its neutrality and the inviolability of its territory. In July, its forces were reorganised, with the appearance of the Tetuán Division (General Joaquín Milans del Boch), the Cazadores Brigade (General Martínez Anido), the Ceuta Infantry Brigade (General Sanchez Majon del Basto) and the 2nd Brigade of the 1st Division (General Ayala Lopez). Generals Aguilera and Primo de Rivera also remained in Africa, while Arráiz de Conderena and Aguado returned to Spain. The reader should take note of General Miguel Primo de Rivera. He was sent to Spain in 1915, reaching the posts of Captain General of Madrid (1921) and Barcelona (1922), entering into politics and being appointed as Senator. He led a hard but effective repression against anarchists and was known for his radical opinions about leaving Morocco, proposing even to swap Gibraltar for Ceuta. Probably he was marked by his hard experience in Africa, and by the death of his brother Fernando,

the hero of the Disaster of Annual. Finally, in 1923, Primo de Rivera, supported by King Alfonso XIII, he became dictator of Spain but, paradoxically, instead of leaving Africa he ended up winning the war.[8]

The Spanish "Barrón Flecha" Aeroplanes

As for the air forces, with the operations focused against the Raisuni, on 29 March 1914 a new airfield was opened in Larache and the Farman squadron from Arcila was moved there. The Arcila aerodrome, and another opened at Alcazarquivir, became auxiliaries to the Larache airfield. With operations almost halted, the pilots devoted themselves to aerial exploits. On 14 February a Nieuport VI-M, plate number 6, of captains Herrera and Ortiz Echagüe took off from Tetouan to greet King Alfonso XIII who was in Seville, achieving the first flight over the Strait of Gibraltar, linking Europe and Africa. On 16 May, the 2nd Squadron left for Melilla, to the new Selouane aerodrome, to provide air support for the eastern area, formed by five pilots and two observers in

The Cuban-born Lieutenant Colonel Alfredo Kindelán Duany, when he was captain in 1913. He would command the aviation in Africa and the Nationalist air forces during the civil war, also becoming a member of the Royal Academy of History. (via Sánchez & Kindelán)

The Nieuport VI-M of Emilio Herrera, the first plane that crossed the Strait of Gibraltar on 14 February 1914, flying from Tetuán to Tablada, Seville. (Archivo Histórico Ejèrcito del Aire via Yusta Viñas)

Captain Barrón in the cockpit of his Barrón Flecha aeroplane, inspired by the Austrian Lohner. (via Sánchez & Kindelán)

Captain José Ortiz Echagüe posing with a Barrón Flecha plane with its typical bat shape wings. (Archivo Histórico Ejèrcito del Aire, via Yusta Viñas)

The Spanish-designed Hispano-Suiza V8, probably the best engine of the First World War. A total of 49,893 units were sold to the Allied powers. Its aluminium alloy blocks significantly reduced the weight of the engines but developed the same power as otherwise similar machines. The company was based in Barcelona, being founded by Mateu Bisa, Seiz Zaya and the Swiss Marc Birkigt. They expanded their facilities to Bois-Colombes, France. Some of the Spanish planes ended up with this engine, or its successors. (via Salas Larrazábal)

four Nieuport VI-Ms. These units were commanded by Herrera (in Selouane), and by Barrón (in Tetuán). Kindelán, the Chief of the Aviation in Morocco since 1914, foresaw that aviation could be used not only for reconnaissance and air support, but also to supply the dozens of isolated positions with munitions, food and ice blocks as a supply of water, as he wrote in 1916. Kindelán was later moved to Madrid and was replaced by Commander Bayo.[9]

With the outbreak of the First World War, it was impossible to acquire new materiel, with the exception of three Morane Saulniers

bought by Lieutenant Ortiz Echagüe. This would encourage the birth of the Spanish air industry. The Farmans would continue in Arcila until 1919 (although according to some data they would be replaced in 1915 by the Farman MF-11s). Half a dozen MF-11s were acquired by Spain, being moved to Arcila under Captain Ángel Pastor. The old Lohners, Moranes and Nieuports in Tetuán and Melilla, were replaced by the Spanish-built "Barrón Flechas", from June 1917, inspired by the Lohner. Eduardo Barrón designed the "Flecha" (Arrow), an aircraft with a Hispano-Suiza 140hp engine, of which 18 units would be produced. Six of them with an older engine, an Austro-Daimler, in Cuatro Vientos, and 12 of them in Escoriaza, Zaragoza, with the excellent Hispano-Suiza. Shortly after, Barrón improved this aircraft with the "W" model, and Captain Sousa designed the AME Mixto, which was manufactured at Cuatro Vientos, Madrid. Nevertheless, the Flechas would be retired in 1919 due to an accident on 12 May 1918, when Captain Zubía and his observer were killed in Tetuán, and as more modern planes became available from the surplus stocks of the First World War. In 1917, the Hispano-Suiza company set up an aircraft factory in Guadalajara, producing DH-6 and later DH-9 trainers that were delivered in 1923 and 1922, respectively. Also, as for combat machines, in August 1919 a batch of 16 De Havilland DH-4 and eight Breguet XIV were acquired for the Spanish air forces. Half of the DH-4s were sent to Tetuán and Larache, with the Breguets being involved in the taking of Xauén, and the other half were sent to Melilla, in September. On 15 August 1919, three heavy Farman F-50 bombers arrived in Tetuán, the first twin-engine plane of the Spanish aviation. In the hands of Captain Sáenz de Buruaga, the F-50 made the first air attack on El Raisuni's forces, continuing to launch ongoing night bombings against the Rifians. One of the F-50s was lost in a trip from Morocco to Seville in June 1920, but in 1923 a new F-50 was bought to replace it. The F-50s were in service until 1924.[10]

El Raisuni, Pro-Spanish

In 1915, the rivalries between the Rifians exploded, and in April the kabyles of Anyera, Beni Ider, Haus and Wad Ras rebelled against El Raisuni and defeated him. At the same time, General Silvestre continued his harassment of El Raisuni in the western zone, taking Regaia, 2km from Zinat. El Raisuni then fled to Tazarut, in the mountains of Beni Aros, north-west of Xauén, but he remained in contact with Lieutenant General Marina. El

General Fernández Silvestre observes El Raisuni's positions in Zinat with his binoculars. (Gárate Córdoba)

An artillery battery under General Jordana, occupying Mount Gazún. Note the dress of the soldiers, wearing the Wolseley salacot and the absence of the "Rayadillo". (via Villalobos)

Raisuni sent his representative to Lieutenant General Marina on 8 May, but he was shamefully assassinated with the participation of Spanish officers. The scandal was enormous. Lieutenant General Marina had to resign, and General Silvestre was appointed as aide to King Alfonso XIII and taken out of Morocco.[11]

The new High Commissioner, General Gómez Jordana, who had come from Melilla, resumed contact with El Raisuni and reached an agreement with him on 25 September. The Moroccan recognised the Spanish government and would receive arms and funds to maintain his own Mehala. El Raisuni would then subdue the rebels and be appointed governor of wherever he conquered, although always under Spanish rule. The Spanish troops would not intervene in the offensive unless they were called on by El Raisuni himself. The first results did not take long to arrive, and with the help of the Moroccan, General Villalba with forces from the Larache Command took Megaret and Maida. Soon after,

Lieutenant Colonel Berenguer in Zoco el Arbaa of Beni Aros, in September 1915. (via Gárate Córdoba)

the Mehala of Raisuni sacked Taguezart, the base of his main rival, conquering the village of Beni Aros. In 1916 the offensive continued, and with the help of El Raisuni, the Spanish took Amerzan, Sidi el-Arbi, Sel-la, Zinat and el Borch, closing the border with the international zone of Tangier to the north, and controlling the whole Wad Ras kabyle. In May, El Raisuni settled with his Mehala in the Fondak, a crossroads between Arcila, Larache, Tangier, Tetouan and Ceuta. There, according to an interview with General Gómez Jordana, his forces amounted to 2,000 warriors (a figure more in line with the reality of the Rifians, instead of the inflated Spanish and French estimates). In all these operations Captain Franco was mentioned prominently as the commander of a company of the 2nd or 3rd Tabor of Regulares. Franco's "baraka" was mentioned again, as he was one of the seven unharmed officers out of the 42 officers of the Regulares. In June, El Raisuni, helped by the Regulares, put an end to the Anyera rebellion, clearing the Ceuta area of enemies. The biggest battle of this period took place there, when General Milans del Bosch, commander of Ceuta, moved to Cudia Federico with 9,500 soldiers in three columns, with a fourth as a reserve. The general marched from there to the Biutz, to close the Anyera gap. In the end, the naval artillery of the battleship *Pelayo*, cruiser *Princesa de Asturias* and gunboats *Bazán* and *Bonifaz* that fired on Punta Altares and Alboaza managed to clear the front of rebels. The Spanish suffered 310 casualties in a hard-fought action, this time including the young Captain Francisco Franco. Franco, attached to Colonel Genova's Half Brigade, attempted to storm the so-called Loma de las Trincheras, where a bullet pierced his stomach. While Franco was in agony for several days, even his parents came from El Ferrol to say goodbye to him, but incredibly, he survived. However, his African days were over … for the moment.

Thanks to these operations, Spain was able to repatriate 28 battalions and three squadrons, totalling some 20,000 soldiers. However, El Raisuni now refused to vacate the Fondak (Wad Ras) centre of communications or to allow troops to be stationed at Alcazarseguer (Anyera) and throughout 1917 and 1918 blocked the construction of the Ceuta–Tetouan road. The tension with the Moroccan was so strong that Gómez Jordana died of a heart attack on 18 November 1918, while writing a letter complaining about his misdeeds. His replacement was General Dámaso Berenguer Fusté, founder of the Regulares.[12]

The capable High Commissioner Gómez Jordana (1915–1918), who died of a heart attack due to workload and tensions with El Raisuni. (Marín Ferrer)

The War Against El Raisuni

General Berenguer broke definitively with the Moorish leader, but first he prepared the ground. In 1919 he accepted the submission of several factions from Anyera, next to Ceuta, which owed obedience to El Raisuni, and also those of Beni Mesauar. His plan was to assault the Fondak de Ain Jedida and occupy all of Wad Ras from there. El Raisuni, seeing himself threatened, proclaimed himself Sultan of Yebala again and returned to his fortress in Tazarut (Beni Aros), a real eagle's nest, south-west of Tetuán. In March 1919, Spanish operations began in the north: the Regulares, the Indigenous Police and several friendly Harkas left Ceuta and began to occupy Anyera, entering Alcazarseguer on the 20th. The Mehala of El Raisuni was defeated at Madan and Beni Salah at the cost of 33 dead. By the end of May the Spanish had sent several converging columns from Zoco El Jemís, Laucién, Tetuán and Cudua Hará, and took all of Anyera and El Haus, securing the Ceuta–Tetouan communications, and threatening Wad Ras from the north and east. Lieutenant Colonel Castro Girona threatened Ben Karrich from Tetuán to distract the Moorish forces. Finally, in July, the kabyle of Beni Said of Yebala (south-east of Tetuán and bordering the region of Gomara), passed to Spain thanks to the efforts of the Jerife el-Darqaui, opening a breach in the rear of the rebels. At the same time, General Barrera began operations against the kabyle of Ahl Sherif, to the south-west, in the Command of Larache, approaching the region of Gomara from the west. Turning to the north, General Barrera obtained the submission of part of Beni Gorfet, and advancing still further he took the gap of Jarrub, west of Beni Ider, allowing communication with Yebel Hebb and Beni Aros, and cutting the line of arms supply that from Tangier reached the base of El Raisuni in Tazarut. All these operations were carried out mainly with the Regulares as a shock force. Throughout 1919 these units had been expanded to four Groups: the 1st, 3rd and 4th of Tetuán, Ceuta and Larache respectively, in the western area, and the 2nd of Melilla, in the eastern area.[13]

Setback in Cudia Rauda

The next step was to invade Wad Ras, the last relevant possession left to El Raisuni in the north, and where the communications centre of El Fondak de Ain Jedida was located. In June 1919, General Domingo Arráiz, of the Ceuta Command, planned an operation in the Zem-Zem mountain range, on the southern border of Anyera, to enter Wad Ras on condition that "there were no European casualties". Therefore, once again the main force would be formed by the Moroccan Regulares with Spanish commanders. The first objective would be the hill of Uesti and the Morabo of Cudia Rauda. Two columns were launched under Colonel Rodríguez del Barrio, from the Sector of Melusa. Commander Cantero's column would depart to the north, and Lieutenant Colonel Canís's column would do so from Sel-la, in the west of the Sierra, with the 3rd Group of Regulares from Ceuta. Lieutenant Colonel Canís occupied Uesti on 11 July, leaving part of his forces there, while a vanguard formed by Indigenous Police and a friendly Harka advanced towards Cudia Rauda. Sadly, these units were confused with the Rifians, so they were cannonaded by the Spanish artillery. On top of that, this noise warned the rebels of the Spanish advance. Meanwhile, Lieutenant Colonel Cantero also managed to crown the Zem-Zem mountain range.

The Spaniards then fortified Cudia Rauda, protecting it with three positions, while the Moors concentrated in the area and shot at the posts. Then, at 1600 hours the Regulares abandoned the position, leaving behind a garrison, but the Miscrela battery blundered and shelled them again on the retreat, causing panic. The friendly Harka was dispersed, some Regulares defected, and Lieutenant Colonel Canís's column was not able to leave the southernmost position of Cudia Rauda. In the other positions, Commander Cantero's column was split in two, and his rearguard had to return to Cudia. Colonel Rodríguez del Barrio himself, commander of all the expedition, advanced in the afternoon and reached north Cudia, to help Lieutenant Colonel Canís, who was now wounded. The firing lasted all night, and in the eastern position the troops panicked when their officers were killed, so they fled to the other posts, abandoning the wounded who were killed by the Moors. At night, the kabyles came closer and were only repulsed by hand grenades. On the 13th, reinforcement columns arrived from Sel-la and Alcazarseguer, and Colonel Rodríguez del Barrio managed to retake east Cudia, recovering the body of his commander, Zabaleta. In the end, the column of General Barrera, coming from the sector of Larache, arrived when the situation was already controlled. The Spanish suffered 198 casualties in this action. As punishment, General Arráiz was replaced in the Ceuta Command by General Silvestre, who was then returning to Morocco.[14]

Taking El Fondak

Despite the setback of Cudia Rauda, the Spanish continued the operations to occupy the Fondak and all of Wad Ras. To do so, 12,000 soldiers were concentrated against 7,000 Moors from El Raisuni. The Spaniards organised two groups of three columns each: the group of Laucién, next to Tetuán, to the east, under General Vallejo (the columns of Sanjurjo, Castro Girona, and a third one in reserve); and the group of Sel-la and Regaia, to the north, under General Silvestre (the columns of Ruiz Trillo, Navarro and Barrera, with forces of Ceuta and Larache). Both groups would converge in the gorges at El Fondak de Ain Jedida on 27 September. General Vallejo, behind an artillery barrage of 30 pieces and with aviation support, dislodged the heights of Harcha with Sanjurjo's column, on the right, and Mount Cónico, with the forces on the left of Castro Girona. The advance was preceded by a vanguard of the Regulares of Tetouan no. 1 and a Jalifian Mehala, almost without casualties. General Silvestre, confronting the bulk of the enemy in the north, behind Cudia Rauda, lost 130 men in his first advance of 5km in Bukurdux and Cudia Dahari. His left, under Ruiz Trillo, skirted the Zem-Zem from the north,

Fondak de Ain Jedida, a crossroads between Ceuta, Tangier, Larache and Tetuán, and one of the main bases of El Raisuni that was conquered by the Spaniards on 10 October 1919. (Fernández Riera)

and his right, under General Barrera, to the south of Telata. On 2 October, General Vallejo resumed the advance occupying Yebel Heddia, 5km east of the Fondak (despite being under a storm but with artillery and air support), and General Silvestre reached Ain Hammu and Dahari, to the west. In the end Silvestre did not use Navarro's reserve column. Then, both groups cleared the flanks of the gorge on 5 October, reaching the heights of Beni Tanit, south of the Fondak, after Castro Girona surrounded the enemy from the east, while Sanjurjo attacked them frontally. To the west, General Barrera occupied Casa Quemada, and Ruiz Trillo advanced to the north from Telata, until he arrived near the Fondak. General Barrera then launched two Tabors to assault the heights of Telaya, a distraction that made it possible for the Jalifian cavalry and the Regulares to enter the Fondak on the 10th. The Raisuni was able to escape, however. In total the Spaniards suffered 246 casualties, but the communications between Tangier, Ceuta, Tetuán and Larache remained open, and the kabyles of Wad Ras, and to the west, Beni Mesauar and Yebel Hebib, surrendered.[15]

Commander Franco, now moved to the Legion, explains to Lieutenant Colonel Millán-Astray the operations made by the new 1st Bandera. (via Gárate Córdoba)

The Fall of Xauén

In 1920 only the remnants of El Raisuni's warriors in the south-east of the Yebala and the west of the Gomara remained to be eliminated. In this last area was Xauén (El Ajmas kabyle), the holy city of the Rif, never trodden by any foreigner and the next objective of General Berenguer. First, he would have to march south from Tetuán, clearing the mountains of the Beni Hosmar kabyle, with its Gorgues massif. On 14 January, Lieutenant Colonel Castro Girona, with troops of the Jalifian Mehala and the Indigenous Police arrived at the top of Gorgues by surprise, suffering only 18 casualties. The next movement was made from the south-west, to surround all the mountains of the Yebala from behind. The 4th Group of Regulares from Larache occupied Beni Issef, west of Xauén. Then, they arranged a base in the Teffer, guarding the mountains and controlling the road from Alcazarquivir to Xauén, from the south. On 25 June, Ben Karrich was reached (Beni

Hosmar kabyle), in the line of march from Tetuán. In September, the final advance on Xauén was organised: the Jalifian Mehala was to the north-east, at the mouth of the River Uad Lau, in Beni Said de Yebala. They would soon be joined by a new experimental unit: the *Tercio de Extranjeros de la Legión española*, or Spanish Legion, under the command of Lieutenant Colonel José Millán-Astray. The 1st Bandera of the Legion was formed, commanded by Major Francisco Franco, and in October the 2nd and 3rd Banderas would be created. Franco, recovered from his wounds, helped his friend, Colonel Millán-Astray, to create the Legion, then returned to Morocco. Again, cleverly, Franco asked to be moved to the most aggressive and efficient unit of the Spanish army but, on the other hand, dramatically increasing the odds of ending the war as a dead man.

Six thousand soldiers from the Larache Command, under General Alfonso Barrera were concentrated in Teffer, to the west

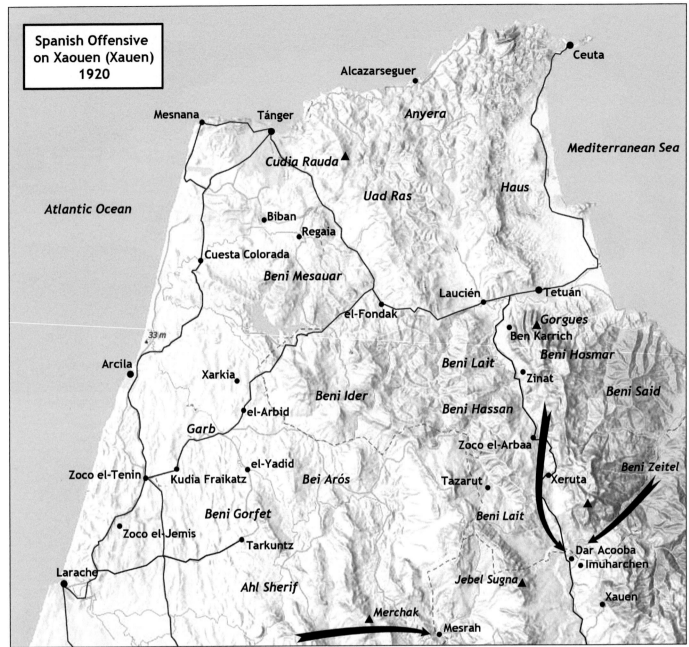

Spanish Offensive on Xaouen (Xauen) 1920

Map of the Spanish offensive to take Xaouen (Xauén) in 1920. (Map by Tom Cooper based on Marín Ferrer)

and two brigades, those of Vallejo and Navarro, which with other reserve forces added another 9,000 men, were grouped in Ben Karrich, to the north. On 20 September seven batteries opened fire, and Vallejo's brigade marched south from Ben Karrich, preceded by the Jarifian Mehala of the Philippine-born Colonel Castro Girona, and the Regulares led by and González Tablas. These forces occupied Zoco el Arbaa, in the north of the Beni Hassan kabyle, on the 28th. This advance forced the surrender of the entire kabyle. General Vallejo entered Dar Akoba and Cheruta, to the south of Beni Hassan, on 4 October. The next step was to move into the kabyle of El Ajmas, now in the Gomara region. Behind this column was General Felipe Navarro's Brigade to cover its rear and the line of communications. On 14 October the Mehala and the 4th Tetuán Group, under Castro Girona, followed by Vallejo's and Navarro's brigades, made the final assault from the heights that dominated Xauén. After suffering 52 casualties, the Spaniard finally entered into the remote, beautiful, legendary and holy city, also known as Chefchaouen.[16]

Tazarut Resists

Further south, however, the kabyle of El Ajmas was also still on the warpath. When the Spaniards abandoned the area leaving only a string of garrisons, such as that of Mura Tahar, the rebels attacked them on 21 October, causing 13 deaths. Meanwhile, in December, the Legion was finally deployed on the front line, with the 1st Bandera remaining at Ouad Laud, the 2nd Bandera at Zoco el Arbaa (Beni Hassan kabyle), and the 3rd Bandera at Ben Karrich. Already in April 1921, a series of operations began from Uad Lau to the north-east, under General Castro Girona to expand the hinterland of Xauén. General Castro Girona had all the Spanish shock forces at hand: the 1st Bandera of Franco's Legion, the Jalifian Mehala, the Mía of the Police of Beni Said and the 3rd and 4th Groups of Regulares from Ceuta and Tetuán. These troops advanced along the Lau River to connect with Xauén from the north-east. On 18 April they advanced 20km along the coast of Gomara, occupying Targa and Tiguisas, in Beni Ziat, and on the 30th they turned south-west again to continue along the river Lau towards Xauén, contacting Sanjurjo's forces, which had

A squadron of Breguet XIVs operating over Beni Aros in 1920. These planes arrived in Tetuán in 1919. (via Villalobos)

Infantry assaulting an enemy position after it has been bombed by the aviation. (via Gárate Córdoba)

At this time, Spain had the following troops in the western zone of the Protectorate: two general commands (Ceuta and Larache); two line infantry regiments (probably Ceuta and Serrallo); 12 Cazadores battalions grouped in two mixed brigades (the 1st, in Tetuán, with the Cazadores battalions of Madrid, Barbastro, Arapiles, Llerena, Segorbe and Talavera; the 2nd, in Larache, with the Cazadores battalions of Catalonia, Tarifa, Las Navas, Figueras, Ciudad Rodrigo and Chiclana); two cavalry regiments; a mixed artillery regiment; two artillery commands (Ceuta and Larache, for position artillery, administrative and non-combat units); three groups of Regulares (1st of Ceuta, 3rd of Larache and 4th of Tetuán); the Tercio of the Legion (1st, 2nd and 3rd Banderas); the Jalifian Mehala; and two friendly Harkas (Alcazar, with 146 men, and Melali, with 346).

departed east from Dar Akoba, in Beni Hassan. On 4 and 5 May, a sortie was made from Xauén itself, taking Mount Mago after suffering 25 casualties, thanks to a flanking manoeuvre made by the Regulares, in which the position of Miskrela was created.[17]

With the capture of Xauén, El Raisuni had been isolated in the north-west (Beni Aros kabyle), in his eagle's nest of Tazarut, and he was completely surrounded by enemies and without any rearguard. General Berenguer did not forget El Raisuni, and he unleashed the final offensive against him. The offensive of May, headed by the 4th Group of Regulares of Larache was very bloody, penetrating in Beni Gorfet, to the west of Beni Aros, which was still rebellious. The Spaniards had to contact several Sheikhs of Beni Aros to obtain their collaboration. Thus, they managed to occupy the sanctuary of Yebel Alam without a fight.

On 25 June the final assault against El Raisuni began concentrically: the 1st Group of Regulares of Tetuán marched from the east, in Xeruta (Beni Hassan), crossing the tiny village of Beni Lait and reaching the Buhaxen peak. They threatened Tazarut from the north and other positions such as those in Buharrax (Beni Ider). The main operation was carried out by the 3rd and 4th Groups of Ceuta and Larache that entered Beni Aros, isolating the natural fortress of Tazarut from its source of supply in the plain, Zoco El Jemís. When the Spaniards were already glimpsing Tazarut, El Raisuni, in desperation, called a truce on 21

July, that was rejected. But before the final assault, some terrifying news came about an unexpected disaster in the east of Spanish Morocco: the entire Melilla Command under General Silvestre had been destroyed in a battle that began in the village of Annual.

General Berenguer immediately held his attack, and he sent as a matter of urgency the Regulares from Ceuta and two Banderas of the Legion (the 1st and 2nd) to Melilla. El Raisuni had been saved again.[18]

5
1920–1921: The Disaster of Annual

While in the western area of the Moroccan Protectorate, Spain cleared the area around Ceuta, Tetuán and Larache of enemies and managed to link these three points together, in the eastern area disaster struck, and the entire Melilla Command was annihilated in a series of battles that began in Annual in 1921. However, to understand what happened it is necessary to go back to 1912, when the Spanish lines were halted at the Kert River after the death in combat of El Mizzián. The new commander of Melilla from 25 December, General Francisco Gómez Jordana, as already seen, preferred diplomatic action rather than military action. So, Gómez Jordana decided first to win the hearts and minds of the Rifians before proceeding with further advances. In the first place, he proceeded to distribute wheat among the population, as they were in great need due to the bad harvests of 1912–1913. On top of that, he began to pay pensions to the rebels of the different kabyles of the interior in order to earn their trust. In this way, the hostility towards Spain diminished and Jordana was able to reduce the strength of many of his positions, to assign almost half of the troops of the sector to attacking columns and thus, he carried out punitive or blockade operations against the kabyles that were still

hostile to Spain, such as Bocoya and Beni Urriaguel, to the west, in the central Rif. These kabyles had attacked the positions of Alhucemas and the Rock of Velez de la Gomera, Spanish islets off the Moroccan coast. Between 1913 and 1914, in the south, General

General Gómez Jordana decorating soldiers in 1914 at the river Kert. (via Gárate Córdoba)

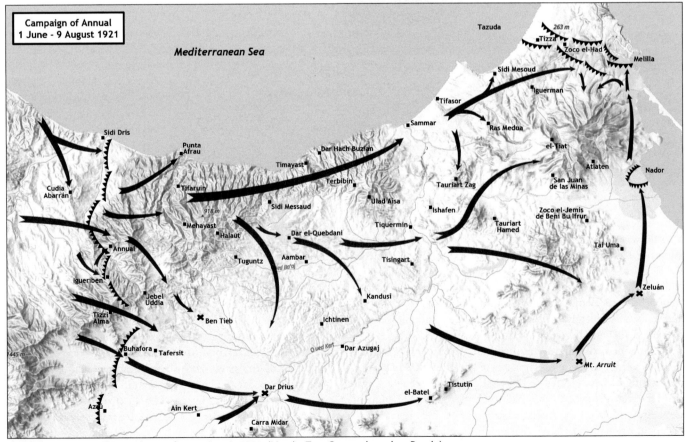
Map of the Disaster of Annual area of operations in 1921. (Map by Tom Cooper, based on Pando)

Jordana expanded his base by occupying Tistutin and Batel (Beni Bu Yahi kabyle), on the Garet Plain, on the road that went through Monte Arruit, advancing to the west and threatening to engulf the Kert River on the south, at its source. In the same way, General Jordana occupied Hassi Berkan, more in the rear, to control the Ulad Settut kabyle, in the upper course of the Muluya River. These operations were carried out almost without casualties.

On 10 May 1915 General Jordana crossed the Kert River and occupied Tikermin, in the central part of the front, entering the formerly hostile Beni Said kabyle. However, it was not all quiet work, for in June the gunboat *General Concha* ran aground off the coast of Bocoya and the kabyles raided the ship, killing 12 crewmen and taking four guns. In any case, in view of his successes, General Jordana was transferred in July to the western zone to deal with El Raisuni, being replaced in Melilla by General Aizpuru. Throughout 1916, General Aizpuru expanded the Spanish positions on the east bank of the Kert River at Tauriat Haman, Tisingart, Kandussi and the Draa Plateau, preventing the Beni Said kabyle from crossing the river. The encirclement of Mount Mauro would begin from the south, from these positions, isolating Beni Said, in the north, from M'talsa, in the south.[1] At the same time, following the policies of the western zone, the native forces were increased. In January 1913, the 7th Mía of the Melilla Indigenous Police was created, and in 1917 a 10th Mía was created. Also, as already seen, in July 1914 the 1st and 2nd Groups of Melilla Regulares were formed, with the 1st, which changed its name to Tetuán, being sent urgently to the western zone, leaving the 2nd Group in the east.[2]

Between 1916 and 1919, with the focus of resources on the west, there were no significant operations in the east. In mid-1919 operations were resumed, and General Aizpuru penetrated further south into the Guerruao (Beni Bu Yahi kabyle), occupying Afso from Batel. Then he turned west, following the bend of the Kert towards its source, taking Reyem and Zoco el-Telata from Ulad Bu Beker (M'talsa), all points on the east bank of the river, threatening to engulf it from the south. After this advance General Aizpuru dominated the whole of the extensive Beni Bu Yahi kabyle. In the central sector, on the other side of the Kert, and with the help of the now allied Kaid Hach Amar, the Spanish occupied Kandussi, Azugaj and Haman (Beni Said kabyle), although still very close to the river. The big boost to the Spanish offensive came when General Aizpuru was replaced by the aggressive General Manuel Fernández Silvestre, who came from the Larache command. His plan was to advance deep from the south to Tafersit, separating like a knife the rebel kabyles of Beni Said, Temsaman, and Beni Ulixek, to the north, from those of Tafersit, M'talsa, and Beni Tuzin, to the south. However, General Berenguer, commander-in-chief of the Protectorate, visited Silvestre and instructed him to first clear his flanks, especially the

right flank to the north, by clearing Mount Mauro, the refuge of the Beni Said rebels.[3]

Silvestre, the Tempest

In May 1920 General Silvestre began his offensive, first to clear his left or southern flank, with several columns. Colonel Riquelme, another future commander of the civil war although on the Republican side, with 2,170 men (7 companies, two of machine guns, from Ceriñola, a Tabor, a Mía of machine guns and a squadron of Regulares, three companies of quartermasters and engineers and two batteries) would advance from Kandussi (Beni Said); Colonel Rodríguez Casademunt, with 2,522 men (a battalion and two machine gun companies of the San Fernando Regiment, a Tabor and a squadron of Regulares, five companies of engineers and quartermasters, and three batteries) would depart from Batel, further south (Beni Bu Yahi); and Colonel Giménez Arroyo, with 2,136 men (a battalion and two machine gun companies of the África Regiment, two Mías and a squadron of Regulares, three companies of engineers and quartermaster, and four batteries) would march from Zoco el-Telata, further south-west (M'talsa). So, Colonel Casademunt's column marched to the south-west, and Colonel Giménez Arroyo's to the north, converging on Haf, and Colonel Riquelme's marched towards Dar Drius, to the east. On the 14th, several columns departed from Batel and Tistutin (Colonel Giménez Arroyo, with five companies of the África Regiment, and a Tabor and a Mía of Regulares; Colonel Monje, with four Indigenous Police companies; and Colonel Ruibal with a machine gun company of the Melilla Regiment, a Tabor of Regulares and a Mía, supported by three other police Mías coming from the east), in Beni Bu Yahi kabyle, to march south and take Afso, in the same kabyle, to improve communications with Zoco el-Telata of Bu Beker, which was further west. On the 15th, Colonel Riquelme's vanguard, formed by Colonel Morales' indigenous troops, took Dar Drius (M'talsa or Beni Ulixek kabyle, depending on the source), an important crossing of the Kert in its curve to the west, a position from which Beni Said was enveloped to the south and deeply. On the 24th, two columns of 7,000 men advanced even further west, to Abadda (Rodríguez Casademunt's Column), Chaif and Ain Kert (Giménez Arroyo's Column, from Haf, in the

General Silvestre, in the middle with a light colour jacket, during the 1920 offensive. (via *Desperta Ferro* magazine)

Spanish soldiers with a Rifian prisoner in the days before the disaster. Note their barracks caps. (via Pando)

Peninsular soldiers on the ground, protecting a truck convoy in Abadda in 1920. (via *Desperta Ferro* magazine)

advance to the north-east like a whirlwind, occupying Dar Quebdani on 10 December, and on the 11th his troops crested the legendary Monte Mauro. Silvestre's advance had been spectacular.[4]

Abd El-Krim Appears

On New Year's Day 1921, the Temsaman kabyle went over to Spain, except for the Trugut faction, close to the hostile Beni Urriaguel kabyle. Its leaders offered to guide Colonel Morales, in Dar Drius, to occupy the whole region up to the sea. Once authorised by General Berenguer (who instead of reprimanding Silvestre took advantage of his good luck and the favourable tide), Colonel Morales' Spaniards (a company of San Fernando, a Tabor and a squadron of Regulares, a company of engineers and a battery) occupied Afrau, on the coast, and marching from the interior, occupied Annual and Izumar (Beni Ulixek kabyle) between 11 and 21 January. After building up his forces, in the next push General Silvestre finally reached Sidi Dris, on the coast, on the border between Temsaman and Beni Said on 12 March. The column of Lieutenant Colonel Núñez del Prado (a Ceriñola company, four Mías, one of machine guns, two squadrons of Regulares, and a battery) advanced to the Amekran River, north-west of Annual, covering the advance of two other columns that would go to Sidi Dris: on the left, that of Colonel Morales himself (eight Mías of Indigenous Police and a battery), and on the right, that of Lieutenant Colonel Marina (five Peninsular companies, two of machine guns, two Mías of Regulares and a squadron). The next step would be to advance towards the Bay of Alhucemas, in the central Rif, to the east, to subdue the kabyle of Beni Urriaguel, the most dangerous and second most populated in the whole Protectorate, perhaps some 4,500 warriors alone. However, Colonel Morales, although optimistic, stated that the Spanish deployment had reached its maximum and that nothing more could be done without reinforcements. General Silvestre, on the other hand, thought that they could still advance as far as the Nekor River, in the middle of the bay. All this advance had been made with almost no opposition from the Rifians, whose only hostile Harka was in Azilaf, to the south-west (but the rest of Beni Tuzin was willing to cooperate in subduing it), and to

south), like an arrow, very close to Tafersit. Thus, the impetuous Silvestre was practically skipping Berenguer's instructions, and his flank-clearing manoeuvre had become the main action he was aiming for. On 5 August, Colonel Giménez Arroyo took Azrú, south of Tafersit, and enveloping it from behind, Colonel Riquelme took Hamuda, entering on the 7th at Tafersit itself, and on the 12th at Azib de Midar. However, this wedge was pinned down, and in the autumn it began to come under pressure from the rebel Tunzi, who had reinforcements coming from the central Rif, from Beni Urriaguel and Temsaman. However, General Silvestre pressed General Berenguer to allow him to turn north and attack Mount Mauro from behind, finishing off Beni Said. General Berenguer finally relented, and on 5 December Colonel Riquelme enveloped the Rifian positions of Ben Tieb (Beni Ulixek kabyle), brilliantly and without casualties, so that the bulk of the kabyle went over to Spain, as did some elements of Beni Said, such as Kaddur Naamar. General Silvestre continued his

Colonel Morales, in the centre, between soldiers of the Policía Indígena. Morales led Silvestre's vanguard but was against advancing further, being killed while trying to cover the withdrawal of the Annual column. (via Pando)

his father, Abd el-Krim El Khattabi, Kaid of Beni Urriaguel, collaborated for a possible Spanish landing in Alhucemas. The Rifians burnt his house and killed his servants, so he had to flee and take refuge in Melilla. However, after two years he was able to return to Axdir, the head village of Beni Urriaguel, where he continued to act as an undercover Spanish agent. One of his sons, Muhammad Abd el-Krim would become the famous Rifian leader. He started working as a Spanish translator, judge and journalist in Melilla. His brother M'hammed studied engineering in Malaga. El Khattabi, with German funds, tried to build a Harka to invade French Morocco, for which his son Abd el-Krim was imprisoned by the Spaniards, to avoid a conflict with Germany. Abd el-Krim then broke his leg when he attempted to escape and was crippled for life. At the end of the First World War he was reinstated, but as he was fearing reprisals for his pro-German actions and being called by his father, he joined him and his brother in Axdir in 1919. Faced with the Spanish advance of Silvestre, El Khattabi tried to organise a defensive Harka but he failed, and he was subsequently poisoned. His son Abd el-Krim was appointed new Kaid, and he managed in January 1921 to unite six kabyles of the central Rif (Beni Urriaguel, Bocoya, Beni Bu Frah, Beni Itfet, Zarkat and Targuist), but the bad harvest weakened his forces, and he penetrated in Temsaman with only 300 warriors, remaining in expectation.[5]

the north-west, in the mountains of Temsaman, in Trugut, being reinforced by Beni Urriaguel Rifians. In April, General Silvestre went on leave for a month, and by the end of May, when he returned, the situation of relative calm was beginning to change. Beni Said and Beni Ulixek kabyles continued to cooperate, but more and more Temsaman elements were joining the Trugut faction, and a new leader, Abd el-Krim concentrated a Harka of 300 to 500 Beni Urriaguel Rifians in Yebel Qama, in Temsaman kabyle, to pressure this kabyle into full rebellion. In the south, the Beni Tuzin men also reinforced their Harka.

For the first time, Abd el-Krim entered the scene, who from being a supporter of Spain became its main enemy. In 1911,

The Massacre of Abarrán

Despite these signs, General Silvestre, confident following positive reports on Temsaman, authorised the advance of the line to Abarrán, on the other side of the Amekran River, already inside Temsaman kabyle. Commander Villar crossed the gorges surrounding Annual with a column of 1,500 soldiers (the 1st Tabor and the 2nd Squadron of Regulares, three Mías of Indigenous Police, two Ceriñola machine gun companies, two of engineers, and a battery) and occupied Abarrán, leaving there 250 soldiers (including 50 Europeans) from a Mía of the Indigenous Police, a company of Regulares and an artillery battery. Then the unthinkable began: the Temsaman warriors who had accompanied Commander Villar, as soon as he turned around, began to fire on the Abarrán position. Commander Villar himself heard the shots, but still returned to Annual. The position was fired upon from a hill and assaulted from the other side, a moment that part of the Regulares took advantage of to defect when the Spanish officers were killed. The artillerymen then fled, and the Moors took the position along with four Krupp pieces and 200 rifles on 1 June.

The next day the Rifians turned north towards the coast and attacked Sidi Dris, but the position held thanks to the fire from the gunboat *Laya* and a party of 17 sailors who landed two machine guns. However, General Silvestre continued to occupy positions,

Abd el-Krim, the very real creator of the Rifian nationalist conscience and movement that was near non-existent before him. He began his days as a friend of the Spanish, ending them as their enemy. (via Pando)

Abd el-Krim seen later during the Rif War. (via Fernández Riera)

Officers and soldiers of the Abarrán post, later overrun and massacred. The second from the left is Artillery Lieutenant Flomesta, captured and then killed. (via Pando)

and on 3 June he occupied Talilit, to the north-east of Annual, to communicate with Sidi Dris, which was resupplied and reinforced with a company of Regulares. South of Annual, General Silvestre occupied Igueriben with two companies of the Ceriñola Regiment and a battery. The problem was that after the triumph of Abarrán the Rifians were increasingly reinforced, now with elements from Beni Ulixek, where Silvestre's own headquarters was located, and from Beni Said itself, further to the north-east, in his rear.[6]

On 15 June, Abd el-Krim's heavily reinforced Harka was concentrated on the east bank of the Amekran River, in a line opposite Bumeyan and Igueriben. This second position, incredibly, had no water, so that every day the so-called Hill of Trees (Loma de los Árboles) had to be occupied, to cover the defenders of the position while they fetched some water. However, on the 16th, the Spaniards found the hill occupied by the Rifians. To expel them, a column of three squadrons and six companies of Regulares, one from Ceriñola and a battery under Colonel Monje Prado left Annual and managed to clear the hill at the cost of 63 casualties. The punishment suffered by the Rifians must have been heavy because the harassment actions ceased for about 15 days, and some elements returned to the central Rif. However, at the beginning of July, the Rifian line stretched further up the Amekran River, from Tafersit in the south to the sea. Now they were some 1,500 warriors.

The Deployment of the Spanish Forces

The Melilla Command had the San Fernando, Ceriñola, África, and Melilla Regiments, with 3,000 soldiers each; the Alcántara Cavalry Regiment, with 1,000 horsemen; the Mixed Artillery Regiment, with 1,500 men; the Artillery Command, with 1,400;

Captain Ramón Huelva, killed when defending the Abarrán post. (via Pando)

Regulares of Melilla in July 1921. A large number of them surprisingly defected in the Disaster of Annual, as happened with those of Abarrán. (via Pando)

An aerial photograph of the Abarrán post, the first to fall in the Disaster of Annual. (via Marín Ferrer)

Table 7: Spanish Forces in Melilla (Annual, July 1921)	
Units	Strength
Melilla Regiment	3,000
África Regiment	3,000
Ceriñola Regiment	3,000
San Fernando Regiment	3,000
Alcántara Cazadores Cavalry Regiment	1,000
2nd Group of Regulares	1,841
Indigenous Police	3,200
Mixed Artillery Regiment	1,500
Melilla Artillery Command	1,400

Table 8: Deployment of Major Garrisons before Annual		
Units	Strength	Location
Five infantry companies, two machine gun companies of San Fernando, seven infantry and one machine gun company of Ceriñola, four infantry companies of África, six Mías of Regulares, three battalions of mixed artillery regiments, HQ of three battalions of Ceriñola, and HQ of three Tabors of Regulares.	5,100	Annual
Four infantry companies, one machine gun company of Melilla, and HQ of one battalion.	950	Cheif (M'talsa)
Two infantry companies of San Fernando, four squadrons and one machine gun squadron of Alcántara, HQ Alcántara Regiment and one battalion.	1,350	Dar Drius (M'talsa)
Four infantry companies, and one machine gun company of the África Regiment.	850	Zoco el-Telata of Bu Beker (M'talsa)
Three infantry companies, and one squadron.	700	Ben Tieb (Beni Said)
Five companies, one machine gun company of Melilla, and HQ of two battalions.	1,200	Dar Quebdani (Beni Said)
One company of Ceriñola, three Mías and one machine gun Mía of Regulares, HQ of one Tabor and Disciplinary Brigade (battalion).	1,050	Nador
One company, one machine gun company, HQ of three battalions and artillery command.	800	Melilla City

the 2nd Group of Regulares of Melilla, with 1,841 soldiers; and the Indigenous Police, with 15 Mías, some 3,200 men. In total there were officially between 24,776 and 25,790 soldiers, depending on the source; 5,020 of whom were natives, and the rest, Spaniards. According to the Picasso File, drawn up as a result of the disaster, there were in fact 20,139 soldiers, with 4,637 absent. Therefore, these figures were theoretical, and would have to be reduced by approximately 20 percent.

In any case, despite these numbers, the Spanish units were scattered in about 45 positions. The main one was that of Annual (in Beni Ulixek), under General Silvestre himself with about 5,100 troops (five companies and two of machine guns of San Fernando, another seven companies and one of machine guns of Ceriñola, four companies of África, six Mías of Regulares and three batteries of the Mixed Regiment of Artillery, and the headquarters troops of three battalions of Ceriñola and three Tabors of the Regulares); the next post was at Cheif (M'talsa), about 20km to the south-east, consisting of some 950 troops (four companies and one of machine guns of the Regiment of Melilla, and a Battalion headquarters); about 1,350 soldiers (two companies of San Fernando and four squadrons of cavalry and one of machine guns from Alcántara, a battalion headquarters and that of Alcántara Regiment) were at Dar Drius (M'talsa), about 10km to the east; about 850 men (four companies and one of machine-gunners from the África Regiment), at Zoco el-Telata of Bu Beker (M'talsa), another 15km further south; about 700 men (three companies and a squadron of different units), at Ben Tieb (Beni Said kabyle), about 10km north-west of Dar Drius; about 1,200 soldiers (five companies and one of machine-gunners from the Melilla Regiment, and headquarter troops from two battalions) at Dar Quebdani (Beni Said kabyle); about 1,050 men (one company of Ceriñola, three Mías of the Tabors and one of machine-gunners of Regulares, and headquarter troops of a Tabor of Regulares and the Disciplinary Brigade) to the east, at Nador, 10km south of Melilla; and finally about 800 combatants (an infantry company and a machine gun company, and the headquarter

Heavy but antiquated artillery from one of the 45 major Spanish positions in the Eastern Rif. (via Pando)

The Taulet post. An example of one of the little Spanish posts that would be overrun in the Disaster of Annual. (via Pando)

troops of three battalions and the artillery command) in Melilla City, with several thousand more due to the high concentration of rearguard services and troops on leave. In fact, according to the Picasso File, up to 6,776 men were grouped in Melilla, and the rest, 13,363 soldiers, were dispersed in the different positions and columns. In turn, the occupied territory was divided into theoretical perimeters, giving Annual to the Ceriñola Regiment, Dar Drius to San Fernando, Kandussi to Melilla, Telata to África, and Nador to the Disciplinary Brigade. Thus, General Silvestre's situation, with a relatively large force in Annual in front of the main enemy Harka, that was smaller in number and less well equipped, was far from desperate. However, although some seven positions had about a thousand men each, there were 38 others with 300 or fewer, and perhaps another 50 with a few dozen soldiers only, many of them without water or in a post surrounded by mountains dominated by the Rifians. Such posts could fall one by one if the general did not react with energy. And General Silvestre did not lack energy.[7]

The Massacre of Igueriben

Igueriben, defended by two San Fernando companies, about 5km south of Annual, and without water, came under attack by the Rifians again on 3 and 4 July. With the access roads dominated by

Commander Benítez led the 247 men of the Igueriben post, which was surrounded and destroyed despite the desperate attempts to relieve him by all the Annual garrison. He was the last to die in the post, on 21 July. (via Pando)

gorges and hills in the hands of the Rifians, their situation was desperate. Even the Hill of Trees that controlled the access to the water was being fortified by Abd el-Krim. On 15 July, the Moors went so far as to erect trenches a mere 1.5km from the position. On the 17th, Igueriben was already surrounded by a Harka coming from Amesauro. Finally, General Silvestre reacted, and on the afternoon of the same day he sent Lieutenant Colonel Marina from Annual with 1,300 soldiers (two squadrons of Regulares, a Tabor of infantry, three companies of Ceriñola and a battery) to the rescue of Igueriben. However, marching slowly due to the convoy of mules with them, they were massacred along the way. Despite this, Captain Cebollino Von Lindeman, another future commander of the Nationalist side during the civil war, with a squadron of Regulares managed to reach Igueriben with 70 mules, supported by a sortie made by Lieutenant Galán from the garrison. However, part of the load was lost on the way, and most of those who arrived, wounded, remained in the garrison, not being able to leave. At night, the Rifians assaulted the position, and the Spaniards, lacking water, had to distribute half a vat of vinegar among the soldiers. On the 18th the Rifians managed to bring their scarce artillery into play and began to bombard Igueriben, and a new attempt to send a second convoy from Annual was repulsed. At night, the Moors were so close that they began to throw hand grenades at Igueriben. On the 19th, General Silvestre launched three columns to save the position: that of Colonel Alfaro, with three companies and three squadrons of Regulares; of Commander López Moreno, with three companies; and of Lieutenant Colonel Núñez del Prado, with two companies, one of machine guns, and another of Regulares. The Rifian fire stopped and forced the Spaniards to fall to the ground, having to retreat without reaching their objective. Meanwhile, the garrison had to undress inside holes to protect themselves from the heat, mash potatoes to drink the juice, and added sugar to ink, cologne and urine to quench their thirst. General Navarro, second in command of the Melilla Command, arrived with reinforcements from the Indigenous Police, but did not dare to attack the Rifian lines, so General Silvestre replied that he himself would lead the attack 'for humanity and dignity'.

On 20th, General Silvestre called up the Alcántara Cavalry Cazadores Regiment to join him in the attack, and his second in command, Lieutenant Colonel Fernando Primo de Rivera (not to be confused with his brother, Miguel, future dictator of Spain), departed on the 21st for Ben Tieb. However, this meant another delay for the rescue forces, and on the 20th the convoy did not depart to help those at Igueriben. Also, a Rifian bomb hit the tent of the seriously wounded, killing them all. On the 21st the final offensive to help Igueriben was launched. General Navarro started it with practically the entire garrison of Annual, but after six hours of fighting he got stuck, so that General Silvestre himself, who brought the Alcántara Regiment with him, took over the command. General Navarro was sent to Melilla for reinforcements. General Silvestre organised three columns, under Colonels Manella,

General Silvestre in the last days of June 1921, the last photo taken of him, probably while he was trying to relieve Igueriben. (via Pando)

A convoy like this one in 1921, tried in vain to relieve the post of Igueriben. (via Pando)

Generals Silvestre (on the left) and Navarro, shortly before the Disaster of Annual. (via Pando)

Morales and Commander Villar, including the friendly Harkas from Beni Said, under Kadur Amar, and from M'talsa, under Burrahay. The idea was to assault the enemy lines behind a strong artillery barrage. However, despite this massive effort the Rifian fire did not gave way, and the Spaniards reached 500 metres from Igueriben. Desperate, Commander Benítez sent a message by heliograph with the following tenor: 'It seems incredible that you let your brothers die, a handful of Spaniards who have sacrificed themselves in front of you'. General Silvestre, his pride wounded, put himself in front of the Alcántara Regiment and prepared for a cavalry charge. However, his subordinates restrained him, and the charge was not made. Benítez, seeing that all was lost, organised a sortie to evacuate the position, while Lieutenant Castro disabled the materiel and then shot himself before Benítez was killed, being the last one to leave. Commander Benítez's men were hunted like ducks, and according to a witness:

the troops … huddled against the door to make a swift run and quickly save the distance that separated them from our water reserve and throw themselves avidly into the water; but from a series of marksmen's posts … our soldiers were hunted down one by one … Some, to avoid the dangerous crowding of the exit, threw themselves over the parapet, but when they jumped over the barbed wire, they died in the same way, shot in their tracks, and their remains are still on the barbed wire, eaten away by the crows, like tattered clothes from which skulls hang.

All the officers, except Lieutenant Casado, who was wounded, captured, and then fled, died in combat, and of the 247 men in the garrison, only 25 made it to Annual. General Silvestre watched this in horror, unable to help them, and collapsed. His requests for reinforcements to General Dámaso Berenguer, sent days before, had not been clear enough, so none were sent. Back in the Annual post, Kaadur Naamar, Kaid of Beni Said, recommended General Silvestre not to retreat, remembering the defeat suffered by El Roghi in 1908, but Silvestre had lost his fighting spirit and ordered all the minor positions to withdraw to the main ones, not a bad measure in itself. In the redeployment, the Alcántara Regiment was sent back to Ben Tieb, in the rear, at the entrance of the gorge that reached Annual.[8]

Silvestre Collapses in Annual

At that time, on 18 July, the garrison of Annual was about 5,000 soldiers: five Ceriñola companies, five from África, five from San Fernando, three batteries of the Mixed Artillery Regiment, three Tabors and three squadrons of Regulares (1,400 men), four Mías of the Indigenous Police (400 soldiers) and the Harka of Beni Said (200 warriors). The position was terrible, in a post surrounded by mountains that could be reached only after crossing a 15km-long gorge that started from Ben Tieb. In the early morning of the 22nd, General Silvestre summoned the main leaders of the units to his tent to inform them that they only had enough ammunition to withstand one attack, 100 rounds per soldier. His plan was to retreat to Ben Tieb, where there was an ammunition depot. He calculated that they would suffer some 1,000 casualties, but by concentrating other columns he could put together a manoeuvre mass of 7,000 soldiers. The meeting was held until 0500 hours, and the plan was accepted, but at 1000 hours he called a new meeting in which he informed that reinforcements would arrive shortly, so it was better to hold out. However, the meeting was interrupted by an aide who reported that the Rifians were already advancing on Annual in three or five parallel columns of some 1,000 or 2,000 warriors each. Panic-stricken, General Silvestre ordered an immediate retreat, which began within barely an hour, at 1100 hours, without a detailed withdrawal plan having been drawn up.[9]

However, the Rifians were not advancing on Annual. The movement observed was only the relief of the lines of vigilance that watched Annual and, in fact, Abd el-Krim was taken by surprise with the retreat of the Spaniards. The retreat, without any organisation, soon turned into a rout. The officers became disengaged from their units, and the patrols that had gone out

General Fernández Silvestre collapsed in July 1921 after his failing to relieve Igueriben. According to some he went mad, leaving his command leaderless, shouting 'run, run, little soldiers, the bogeyman is coming', and shooting himself. Painting by Gamonal. (La Esfera, via Pando)

in the morning to bring water to the camp were stunned to see their comrades abandoning it, leaving them to their fate. First, the wounded came out on mules dragging stretchers, with some escorts, then the artillery and machine guns, but as soon as they passed the Regulares' camp outside, they began to be shot at. The sections that were to protect the retreat abandoned their posts and joined the fugitives. The friendly Harkas, wanting to cross the gate, shot at the soldiers who were crowded at the exit, and the indigenous troops, seeing the chaos, defected to the Rifians and began to shoot at the Europeans. Meanwhile, what was Silvestre doing? He had disappeared. There are different versions of his end, although all agree that instead of leading the retreat, he was left alone wandering in Annual. Alongside him were Kaadur Naamar, Kaid of Beni Said, and Colonels Marina and Maella, until the enemy fire dispersed them and finished off the general at the exit of the camp. According to others, more pathetically, Silvestre lost his head and mumbled with his pistol in his hand: 'Run, run, little soldiers, the bogeyman is coming', he then entered his tent and shot himself in the head. And so General Silvestre ended his days: the impetuous one, bold in times of fortune, but emotionally unstable and inert when everything went wrong. 'Like a tempest' as El Raisuni said, the Spaniard had gone too far: 'I, like the sea, am never out of my place, and you, like the wind, are never in yours.'[10]

The Last Charge of the Alcántara Regiment

The retreating Spanish forces, forming a long column, were marching south-east across the plain towards Ben Tieb, with no flanking troops or rearguard to cover the retreat. With the defection of the Moroccan soldiers, at a stroke they had gone from 5,000 to only 3,000 soldiers, and the Rifians, already perfectly equipped, from 1,500 to 3,500. After marching 4km the Spaniards entered a gorge 15km long, going either by the Izumar track, a road that went halfway up the mountainside, or by the main road that went along the bottom of the ravine. On the road below were the mules and wagons of the convoy escorted by the San Fernando Regiment. Panic increased, and many soldiers abandoned their equipment and ran out, only to be crushed by the wagons and mules which also came racing out and up the road above. As the two columns came together chaos ensued. With the left flank being shot at, however, on the right flank Commander Llamas with some loyal Regulares kept their cool, got off the road and covered the withdrawal, advancing parallel to the road but away from it, saving the situation by getting the column over the Izumar slope. The Annual Corps had already lost 700 soldiers, apart from the desertions of the bulk of the Regulares and the Indigenous Police. Colonels Morales and Manella had remained in the rear with a handful of soldiers covering the retreat, ending up dead on the fateful Izumar slope. Meanwhile, at Ben Tieb, Lieutenant Colonel Primo de Rivera and the Alcántara Regiment knew nothing of the escape, when they saw the first truckloads of wounded arrive, and then the bulk of the column. Lieutenant Colonel Primo de Rivera then took the 2nd Squadron and personally led it, together with the machine gun squadron, to the Izumar slope to cover the retreat, but the Rifians were already gone, so they returned to Ben Tieb. There was enough ammunition there to defend themselves, but the fugitives, after drinking water and recovering, abandoned the position. Desperate, Ben Tieb's three companies and a squadron blew up the ammunition depot and joined the march. Now they were not only harassed from the rear but also from the flanks, as the natives of Beni Ulixek, Tafersit and M'talsa, on seeing the

Colonel Morales, killed together with Colonel Manella on the Izumar slope while trying to cover the chaotic withdrawal of the Annual column after General Silvestre disappeared. (via Pando)

Colonel Manella, who was killed with Colonel Morales when covering the Annual retreat. (via Pando)

Picture from Agustín, June 1921, titled "Retiring a Wounded Soldier". Note the large hat or *chambergo*. (La Esfera, via Pando)

Spaniards fleeing, stopped what they were doing and ran to get their carbines to shoot them to see what booty they could get.[11]

General Navarro arrived at Dar Drius, on the eastern border of M'talsa, from Melilla crossing the Kert River, to try to organise a line of resistance there on the 22nd at 1700 hours. Meanwhile, the bulk of the 2,700 soldiers from Annual and Ben Tieb arrived at Dar Drius, without weapons, commanders or ammunition. Seeing their disastrous state, and fearing that the retreat route to Batel, in Beni Bu Ifrur, to the east, would be cut off, General Navarro, after letting them rest that night, joined Dar Drius's two companies to the main body, and continued the retreat on the 23rd, sending the remains of the Regulares, the impedimenta and the trucks of the wounded ahead. Only one unit still maintained its composure: the Alcántara Cavalry Cazadores Regiment, which despite having the name of a medieval Military Order had never shown an outstanding performance, but here it would cover itself with glory. At 0700 hours, under the command of Lieutenant Colonel Primo de Rivera, the 5th and 4th Squadrons covered the retreat of the small garrisons that surrounded Dar Drius (such as Ain Kert and Ababda, to the south-west and west respectively), defending the watering holes and the arrival of the last fugitives from Annual.

At 4km from Dar Drius, overtaking the remnants from Annual, they charged, driving out the Rifians who were harassing them, supported by an artillery battery escorted by elements of San Fernando. At 0800 hours they were informed that the Cheif position, west of Dar Drius, defended by five companies, was surrounded by the enemy, and shots were still heard at Ain Kert (defended by one company), and Carra Midar, even further away, both to the south-west. Lieutenant Colonel Primo de Rivera sent the 5th and part of the 4th Squadrons to Ain Kert. He sent the 3rd and part of the 1st Squadron to Carra Midar. Finally, he personally led the rest of the regiment to Cheif. At this last post, Lieutenant Colonel Romero's troops had already abandoned their position to join the troops from Dar Drius, when they were surrounded by the Rifians. When they had already suffered 125 casualties, the fire suddenly ceased: the Alcántara Regiment had arrived. Lieutenant Colonel Primo de Rivera dismounted his machine guns and part of the 4th Squadron, and with their covering fire the rest charged the Rifians, overrunning them. They had just saved the entire Cheif garrison, some 850 men, who arrived safe and sound. Lieutenant Colonel Primo de Rivera himself exclaimed: 'How well these guys have been able to charge!'[12]

The men of the Alcántara were then sent in the direction of Uestia, a little to the east, to escort the trucks carrying the wounded. However, the trucks accelerated and left the horsemen behind. Then, shouts and gunfire began to be heard: the Rifians had overturned three trucks, and cut the road by noon, killing the wounded. 'The squadrons advanced at a trot, crossing that terrain full of small ravines … The people were animated, reflecting in their faces the desire to meet the enemy, ready to reach for

The riders of the Alcántara Cazadores Cavalry Regiment, ready to charge. This modest regiment, with the name of an old Military Order of cavalry but a rather discreet past, went on to glory by being the only unit that kept its composure during the Disaster of Annual, covering the retreat of its comrades until their total annihilation. (La Esfera, via Pando)

Artillerymen, along with the cavalry and elements of San Fernando, were the only units that fought until the end at Annual as they covered the last charge of the Alcántara Regiment. (via Pando)

their sabres … the bugle of orders sounded (at a gallop), the Rgt advanced swiftly to close in on the convoy'. The charge destroyed the Rifians, killing about 70, dispersing the others, and unblocking the road, but the Alcántara lost 50 men. The regiment continued its escort march to Batel, resting then. Next, Lieutenant Colonel Primo de Rivera discovered that Dar Drius was being set on fire and abandoned, so General Navarro ordered them back to clear the road for the retreat: the Rifians had concentrated in the dry riverbed of the Gan or Igan River, blocking the road to Melilla. Exhausted, Lieutenant Colonel Primo de Rivera deployed his horsemen: only 226 remained. First the machine gun squadron climbed to an elevation and covered the line of the horsemen. The artillery was also deployed to support the charge. Primo then formed a line as his soldiers fell back motionless in the face of the enemy fire. The Lieutenant Colonel then made the final harangue: 'Soldiers, the hour of sacrifice has come, let each one do his duty. If you don't do it, your mothers, your girlfriends, all Spanish women, will say that we are cowards. We are going to prove that we are not'. And they charged, again and again, across the riverbed, clearing every hill, until the way was open. In this last action 181 horsemen and all 226 horses were killed and the rest were wounded. The 13 buglers of the regiment were killed. Lieutenant Colonel Primo de Rivera himself lost his horse but survived. In all, for the whole day, out

of 691 horsemen they suffered 541 killed, five wounded and 78 prisoners: only 67 men remained. The regiment had disappeared, but had earned the Laureate and the glory, and what is most important, General Navarro's fugitives could continue their march to hell.[13]

The Massacre of Monte Arruit

In the meantime, General Navarro was attacked as he crossed the river Kert and its tributary, the Gan. Navarro used his artillery to contain the Rifians, but without soldiers to protect it, once the Alcántara was destroyed, all ended up in the hands of the Rifians. In any case, the fugitives reached Batel, where they remained resting until 29 July. Having exhausted his supplies, General Navarro marched further north-east, to Monte Arruit, on the eastern border of Beni Bu Yahi kabyle, near Beni Bu Ifrur. Shortly before arriving, about 1km from the fort, some Rifians with white flags appeared. Then, suddenly, the Indigenous Policemen of the column went over to the enemy and opened fire against the Spaniards. At the same time, from both flanks other kabyle men appeared from some prickly pears and riddled them with bullets. Again, the column disbanded, abandoning the wounded and artillery, and the remnants entered Monte Arruit. The vanguard, which had not suffered this attack, reacted and some troops from San Fernando bayonetted and drove the Rifians out. In the rear, General Navarro was left alone with the General Staff and Lieutenant Colonel Primo de Rivera. Primo caught a horse galloping loose and gave it to the general to escape, and then he entered Monte Arruit, the last one. The column had been reduced to only 900 soldiers, 150 men falling on the way, but with the wounded and other escapees already at Monte Arruit, the total force now stood at 3,017 men. General Navarro did not lose heart and began to organise the defence, setting up a perimeter, but the best units only had 55 rounds per head and no water or cannon,

Spanish forces in Nador, near the church. The village surrendered but this time the Rifians under Ben Hamed honoured his word and the soldiers' lives were spared, being permitted to move to Melilla. (via Marín Ferrer)

A convoy with wounded soldiers, with injured men being carried on either side of a donkey. (via Marín Ferrer)

retreat to Melilla, a promise that the Kaid Hamed-Ben Hamed kept. However, in Selouane, with its airfield, the Rifians broke their word, and their 530 men (a squadron, a Tabor and a company) were killed once they surrendered. First the Regulares of the cavalry Tabor defected, and the airfield was isolated with only 20 defenders. Even so, Ensign Maroto managed to set fire to the six DH-4 planes of the 2nd Squadron stationed there and prevent them from being captured before surrendering.

On 9 August, finally, General Navarro surrendered his troops at Monte Arruit, some 3,000 men surrounded by 5,000 Moors with artillery, captured from the Spanish, from Kaids Ben Chelal, Buharray, Abd el-Kader and Sidi Hassan. Although the general and officers were taken prisoner, once pushed away from the barracks, again the Moors broke their word, and General Navarro began to hear deafening shouting: first the wounded were killed as they were leaving, and then those inside as they were handing in their weapons. Some troops from the África Regiment who still carried their weapons were able to defend themselves until they all fell, which extended the killings. Ben Chelal's Rifians apologised, saying that the killers were the Beni Urriaguel men, over whom they had no command. However, those of Abd el-Krim said, on the contrary, that their instructions to respect the lives of the soldiers were not obeyed. Although the slaughter stopped, when the survivors left, it continued outside when they were exiting, surrounded and fusilladed by two files of Rifians: in the end the 3,000 soldiers who were assembled there were atrociously killed by stabbing, stoning or shooting. Only 10 chiefs and officers and 50 soldiers escaped alive. General Navarro tried to join his men and suffer their fate, but the Moorish escort prevented him from doing so. The remains of the Spaniards would still be there, scattered across the countryside, several months later. One of these corpses was the one of Lieutenant Colonel Fernando Primo de Rivera, the hero of the Alcántara Cavalry Regiment. His end was rather bitter: on 6 August, he was struck by an artillery projectile in his arm, in Monte Arruit, three days before the surrender. The surgeon had

just a machine gun. Soon, the kabyles surrounded Monte Arruit when the whole Guelaya rose up in arms. General Berenguer, who had arrived in Melilla a few days earlier, informed General Navarro on 31 July that he had no troops to help him, so he authorised him to surrender. Although on the 24th two Banderas of the Legion had landed in Melilla, the 1st under Franco and the 2nd under Fontanés, these troops were destined to defend Melilla. General Sanjurjo also arrived and went on to direct operations, establishing a defensive line from Cape Tres Forcas to the edge of the Gourougou and the Mar Chica.[14]

Meanwhile, all the positions of the Melilla Command except Monte Arruit, Selouane, Nador and Melilla City had fallen. On 2 August Nador surrendered. Its forces, 206 men but with only 70 rifles, with two women and two children, were allowed to

The entrance arch of Monte Arruit post. Here some 3,000 Spaniards would be assassinated once they had surrendered. Others survived but were brutally tortured, having their ears cut off and being forced to eat them. (via Marín Ferrer)

General Navarro, who tried to lead the withdrawal of the leaderless Annual column until being surrounded and captured in Monte Arruit. Then released, he would lead the quieter Ceuta sector. (via *Desperta Ferro* magazine)

A drawing of Ben Chelal, Kaid of the Beni Bu Ifrur, who was forced to enter into an alliance with Abd el-Krim. He saved the life of General Navarro, but it is debatable whether his or el-Krim's men slaughtered the 3,000 Spanish prisoners in Monte Arruit. (via Marín Ferrer)

to amputate his arm without anaesthesia, and Fernando died shortly thereafter from gangrene. His own soldiers buried him in Monte Arruit, and his body was not recovered until 24 October. Primo de Rivera was posthumously awarded the Laureate and is listed as Lieutenant Colonel no. 1 of the Spanish cavalry.[15]

Twenty Years of Roses for Intermedia A

The disaster that befell the 150km main line of march of the fugitives from Annual has been recounted, but the disaster included up to 100 minor dramas, almost one for each position. Back on 21 July, when the Annual garrison abandoned its post in a hurry, it forgot to evacuate, or at least notify, surrounding garrisons of its departure. One of them was Intermedia A, in Peña Tahurda, at the exit of the gorge, south-east of Annual. It was formed by 84 soldiers from San Fernando, astonished as they watched the march of the whole army. As nobody gave them any instructions they stayed in their position. On the 24th, Captain José Escribano, seeing a column of smoke over Dar Drius, far to the rear, understood that they had been abandoned, and tried to evacuate the position, but the enemy fire prevented it. The Rifians had arrived. For three days they withstood the enemy fire, but on the 27th, without water and almost no ammunition, Escribano went out to agree to surrender. However, while they were talking, the Rifians began to advance and to raise the barbed wire stakes, so Escribano ordered to fire even though he was in front of them. The captain was killed in the shooting and the Rifians stormed the position, killing all the garrison except for one deserter. Fifty-six years later, and for nearly two decades, someone sent roses to the position, every year. It was Rosa Margarita Barceló, the fiancée of the young Lieutenant Antonio Medina de Castro, in command of the artillery of the Intermedia A. Antonio's body was found at the foot of his cannons, defending the post, three years later. The Lieutenant wrote to her almost every day until the final battle. In his last one, kept by Margarita, he said: 'and it occurred to me to look at the sky. My gaze went to the stars, and my soul to you … I love you, my beautiful one, my chiquitina [little one], I love you'. Margarita never forgot him, she emigrated to the United States and remained single, remembering the young Antonio. At the age of 77 she was able to visit Peña Tahurda and laid there a bouquet of roses, sending one every year until her death in 1991.[16]

Meanwhile, going back to 21 July, General Navarro ordered Colonel Silverio Araujo Torres to take the column from Kandussi, about 15km north of Dar Drius, further north-east, to Dar Quebdani, in the middle of Ben Tieb's kabyle. Thus, Colonel Araujo joined his two companies to the six based at Dar Quebdani, adding 996 men from the Melilla and África Regiments. There, he remained stationary until the kabyles of Beni Said rebelled when they learned of the disaster and cut off his water supply. The colonel, instead of throwing them out, simply paid them to allow him to be supplied, but despite this undignified gesture, the troops remained without water. Finally, on July 25, Kaadur Naamar,

Colonel Silverio Araujo Torres, who led a 996-man column from Kandussi to Quebdani, surrendering it without fighting and paid money to save their lives. All members of the column were killed, and Araujo prosecuted by court martial. (via Marín Ferrer)

Kaid of the kabyle, offered to save their lives if they surrendered and gave them all their money, and Araujo accepted. However, once they were disarmed, it is not known if, in the confusion and against the kaid's intention, the Rifians began to shoot the soldiers, killing all of them except the commanders. The colonel was imprisoned, and later in Spain condemned in a Council of War with dishonour.[17]

The southernmost position of the Spanish perimeter was Zoco el-Telata de Bu Beker, in M'talsa kabyle, about 15km south of Dar Drius. There were 60 horsemen of the Alcántara Regiment, the 2nd Battalion of África (five companies), the 9th Mía of Police and a battery, adding up to 1,000 soldiers under Lieutenant Colonel García Esteban. Esteban assumed that something serious was happening when the supply convoy did not arrive on the 22nd, and on the 23rd he lost telegraph contact. That night the entire native Mía disappeared. Meanwhile, the heliographers from the nearby minor positions of Haj o Haf (one company), Tixera, Arreyen (one company), Loma Redonda (one company), to the east, some 500 men in all, kept flashing for help. Esteban ordered them to retreat to Zoco el-Telata, arriving on the 24th to only 100 survivors, with the rest dead. Batel post, to the east, being 70km away, and the French zone about 20km to the south, Lieutenant Colonel Esteban decided to retreat into Gallic territory, in the middle of the fog, in the morning at 0330 hours. After 10km the

column was detected, so the Alcántara elements were again in the rear covering the retreat. Next to the French zone, in a gorge, they came under heavy fire. Finally, 467 soldiers arrived at Camp Berteaux out of the 1,100 that had departed.[18]

The Eastern Aviation, Annihilated

To understand the situation of the aviation in Annual it is necessary to go back a few years. The genesis of the air forces in Melilla took place with the creation of Selouane aerodrome and the arrival of the 2nd Expeditionary Squadron in May 1914, with four Nieuport VI-Ms, under the orders of Herrera. Later, these aircraft were replaced by the Spanish-designed Barrón Flecha aircraft in June 1917, and in May 1919 a batch of six new Barrón "Ws" were sent to Tetuán, but they were retired before the end of the year. Once the Great War was over, three twin-engine Farman F-50 bombers were purchased, one of them arriving on 1 August 1919 at Tetuán, in the western sector. Later, in September, eight Breguet XIV A.2s (the reconnaissance version with a Renault engine) were acquired, and also 16 De Havilland DH-4s. The Breguets arrived at Tetuán in October by ship, except for that of Lieutenant Carlos Morenés Carvajal, which flew direct from Cuatro Vientos, Madrid, a remarkable achievement, opening this new air route. With the DH-4s, equipped with a Rolls-Royce engine, a squadron was organised for Melilla, while Tetuán and Larache formed mixed Breguet and DH-4 squadrons. The older samples were being retired, such as the MF-7s from 1915, the Nieuport VI-Ms and Lohners from June 1917, as was probably the case with the MF-11s, the Barrón Flechas and Barrón Ws at the end of 1919, some of them being destined for training in Madrid. The Tetuán and Larache squadrons supported the western front campaigns, and soon the Melilla Squadron would do the same with Silvestre's offensive, with eight DH-4s under Captain Pío Fernández Mulero. Some 45 DH-4 planes in all were deployed in Morocco during the war, forming the "De Havilland Rolls Squadron", and later the "Rolls Group", due to its Rolls-Royce "Eagle" engine. Thirteen DH-4 samples were downed by enemy fire, and 21 lost for other reasons. The survivors were retired in 1927, at the end of the war.[19]

At the time of the disaster at Annual the Melilla Squadron had five DH-4s (perhaps the other three had been withdrawn for repairs or moved to another front). On 23 July, Captain Río Fernández Mulero's squadron bombed the Rifians at Tugunt, observing the chaos in the Spanish lines from the air. They did not know that when they landed the rebels were already besieging Selouane and its airfield, 1km away. Defended by only 43 soldiers, the airfield would fall, so Ensign Maroto ended up destroying the aircraft so that they would not fall into the hands of the Rifians. In one fell swoop, Spain had lost all its aviation in the eastern zone.

The problem was also that the whole Melilla area was very mountainous, so, except for Selouane, there was no land suitable for another airfield until it was decided to use the Hippodrome. On 29 July two planes landed there, a civilian Bristol Tourer piloted by captains Manzaneque and Carrillo, and a DH-4 piloted by captains Moreno Abella and Beda, which crashed and

Type	Number of aircraft	Zone/ Squadron	Notes
Farman F-50	Three	Tetuán	One lost in June 1921
Breguet XIV A.2	Eight	Tetuán Squadron and Larache Squadron	Mixed squadrons with DH-4s
DH-4	Eight	Tetuán Squadron and Larache Squadron	Mixed squadrons with Breguet XIVs
DH-4	Eight	Melilla Squadron	Down to five at the time of the Disaster of Annual, all destroyed at Selouane

Table 9: The Air Forces in Morocco (1919–1921) before Annual (Commander Bayo)

A Breguet XIV with a Spanish made Hispano-Suiza 8Fb engine, allegedly the best engine during the First World War. This sample under Lieutenant Carlos Morenés Carvajal flew directly from Madrid to Tetuán for the first time. (via Sánchez & Kindelán)

Soldiers carrying Carbonit aviation bombs, first imported, and then manufactured in Seville from 1914. Behind is a DH-4 that arrived in 1919. (Archivo Histórico Ejèrcito del Aire, via Sánchez & Kindelán)

The Butcher's Bill

The Disaster of Annual had been consummated, and between this post and Melilla lay the unburied bodies of some 8,000 Spaniards, not counting the wounded, the thousands of native defectors (perhaps as many as 4,000), and some 500 prisoners, making a total of some 13,000 casualties. All of this was thoroughly studied in a parliamentary Commission of Inquiry known as the Picasso File. As a poor consolation, 3,098 soldiers reported missing arrived in Melilla over the next few days, although most of them must have been wounded, so the total casualties would not vary substantially. In addition, the Rifians had seized 100 pieces of artillery. Thus, if in barely a year Silvestre had conquered more territory than Spain had in the last 11 years, Abd el-Krim had destroyed all the Spanish conquests in two months, and Madrid had returned to its 1908 lines in the Melilla sector. Also, Melilla City, nearly empty of forces, looked like a ripe fruit close to falling.[21]

broke down. Thus, for four days the Bristol remained as the only air force available, with Manzaneque and Carrillo supplying the encircled Monte Arruit and Selouane with 50kg loads per trip. Finally, on 2 August, the squadron organised in Tetuán under Captain Sáenz de Buruaga landed with five DH-4s, which began to operate immediately. On the other hand, Maura's government reacted quickly and with budgetary funds and donations received as popular support after the horrors of Annual, some 40 DH-4s and DH-9s were purchased or contracted to be manufactured by Hispano-Suiza (though the DH-9s remained in Spain as trainers until 1927, when a squadron was formed in Melilla), as well as eight DH-9As manufactured in Guadalajara. These examples began to be delivered in 1922. To encourage donations, the purchased aircraft were named after the provinces that had financed them. Another batch of Breguet XIV A.2s was acquired in 1921, this time with the much worse Fiat engine, which had caused a large number of accidents. A batch were also manufactured in Seville, Spain, fitted with a Rolls-Royce engine. The Breguet was one of the types most widely used during the war, with at least 18 of them downed by the Rifians (including the last of the war, in 1927), and some 12 more were also destroyed by accident.[20]

Bibliography

(All in Spanish unless noted otherwise)

Books

Bueno, José María, *Soldados de España* (Valladolid: Alcañiz Fresno, 2011)

Carrasco García, Antonio, and de Mesa Gutiérrez, José Luis, *Las Tropas de África en las Campañas de Marruecos* (Madrid: Almena Ediciones, 2000)

Courcelle-Labrousse, Vincent, and Marmié, Nicolas, *La Guerre du Rif* (Tallandier, 2008) (French)

Fernández Riera, Vicente, *Xauen 1924* (Madrid: Almena, 2013)

Marín Ferrer, Emilio, *Atlas Ilustrado de las Guerras de Marruecos* (Madrid: Susaeta)

Nicolle, Dr David C, and Ali Gabr, Air Vice Marshal Gabr, *Air Power in the Arab World, Vol 4* (Warwick: Helion, 2021) (English)

Pando, Juan, *Historia Secreta de Annual* (Madrid: Temas de Hoy SA, 1999)

Permuy López, Rafael A., *Los Pilotos de Caza de la Aviación Republicana, Vol 1* (Valladolid: Quirón, 2001)

Salas Larrazábal, Jesús, *Guerra Aérea, Vol 1* (Madrid: IHCA, 1999)

SHM (Servicio Histórico Militar), *Historia de las Campañas de Marruecos, Tomo IV* (Madrid: SHM, 1991)

Velarde Silió, Jaime, *Aviones Españoles del Siglo XX* (Fundación Infante de Orleans, 2008)

Villalobos, Federico, *El Sueño Colonial* (Barcelona: Ariel, 2004)

Articles

Albi de la Cuesta, Julio, 'La Noche Triste', *Desperta Ferro Contemporánea*, 30 (Madrid: Desperta Ferro, 2018)

Albi de la Cuesta, Julio, 'Preludio de Alhucemas', *Desperta Ferro Contemporánea*, 11 (Madrid: Desperta Ferro, 2015)

De La Rocha, Carlos, Maps in 'El Desastre de Annual' and 'El Desembarco de Alhucemas', *Desperta Ferro Contemporánea*, 30 and 11 (Madrid: Desperta Ferro, 2015 and 2018)

De Mesa Gutiérrez, José Luis, 'El Desembarco de Alhucemas', *Desperta Ferro Contemporánea*, 11 (Madrid: Desperta Ferro, 2015)

Gárate Córdoba, José María, *España en sus Héroes*, Special, 4, 7, 9, 11, 14, 15 and 16 (Madrid: Ornigraf, 1969)

Madariaga, María Rosa de, 'La República del Rif', *Desperta Ferro Contemporánea*, 11 (Madrid: Desperta Ferro, 2015)

Miguel Francisco, Luis, 'Morir en Monte Arruit', *Desperta Ferro Contemporánea* 30 (Madrid: Desperta Ferro, 2018)

Muñoz Bolaños, Roberto, 'La Derrota de Abd el-Krim', *Desperta Ferro Contemporánea* 11 (Madrid: Desperta Ferro, 2015)

Muñoz Bolaños, Roberto, 'La Ofensiva de Fernández Silvestre', *Desperta Ferro Contemporánea* 30 (Madrid: Desperta Ferro, 2018)

Nogueira Vázquez, Carlos, 'Tácticas de Infantería en la Guerra de Marruecos', *Desperta Ferro Contemporánea* 11 (Madrid: Desperta Ferro, 2015)

Pando, Juan, 'El Desastre de Annual', *Historia* 16, 243 (Madrid: Información e Historia, 1996)

Sánchez Méndez, José and Kindelán Camp, Alfredo, 'La Aviación Militar Española en la Campaña de Marruecos 1909-1927', *Aeroplano Especial*, 29 (Madrid: IHCA, 2011)

Yusta Viñas, Cecilio, 'La Aviación Militar Española, Nacimiento y Desarrollo Inicial', *Aeroplano Especial*, 29 (Madrid: IHCA, 2011)

Web Pages

Anuario Militar, <http://hemerotecadigital.bne.es/results.vm?q=parent%3A0026917454&lang=es&s=23>, accessed September 2021

Notes

Introduction

1 Federico Villalobos, *El Sueño Colonial* (Barcelona: Ariel, 2004), pp.11–15, and his Map no. 1.
2 Federico Villalobos, pp.15–27.
3 Federico Villalobos, pp.29–35.
4 Federico Villalobos, pp.36–42.
5 Federico Villalobos, pp.43–49.

Chapter 1

1 Emilio Marín Ferrer, *Atlas Ilustrado de las Guerras de Marruecos* (Madrid: Susaeta), p.71.
2 Emilio Marín Ferrer, pp.64 and 99. José María Bueno, *Soldados de España* (Valladolid: Alcañiz Fresno, 2011), pp.109, 111, and 259.
3 Carlos Nogueira Vázquez, 'Tácticas de Infantería en la Guerra de Marruecos', *Desperta Ferro Contemporánea,* 11 (Madrid: Desperta Ferro, 2015), pp.24–25.
4 Carlos Nogueira Vázquez, p.26. Antonio Carrasco García and José Luis de Mesa Gutiérrez, *Las Tropas de África en las Campañas de Marruecos* (Madrid: Almena Ediciones, 2000), p.72.
5 Antonio Carrasco and José Luis de Mesa, p.53. Carlos Nogueira Vázquez, p.26. Emilio Marín Ferrer, pp.90 and 92. Mistrust of the Regulares in Villalobos, pp.132–133, citing Ramos Winthuyssen.
6 Antonio Carrasco García and José Luis de Mesa Gutiérrez, p.82.
7 Antonio Carrasco García and José Luis de Mesa Gutiérrez, pp.89–91.
8 Carlos Nogueira Vázquez, p.26. Antonio Carrasco García and José Luis de Mesa Gutiérrez, pp.14–15. José María Gárate Córdoba, Special issue, for the friendship of both commanders and Franco's collaboration. It is generally said that there were less than 10 percent of foreigners in the Tercio, but this is not correct: in 1922 there were 1,107 versus 5,682 Spaniards, and in 1930, 4,034 foreigners from a total of 24,521 soldiers.
9 Carlos Nogueira Vázquez, pp.26–29.
10 All the data have been gathered by the author, consulting several orders of battle, and mainly the ones of 1913–1916, 1922 and 1926 in the *Anuario Militar*.
11 Villalobos mentions 650,000 Rifian inhabitants at the beginning of the century, and 850,000 in the 1950s (according to the Spanish census), resulting in an estimate for about 750,000 in the 1920s. José Sánchez Méndez and Alfredo Kindelán Camp, in 'La Aviación Militar Española en la Campaña de Marruecos 1909-1927', *Aeroplano Especial*, 29 (Madrid: IHCA, 2011), p.71, mention 763,000 inhabitants. Despite the information from the Spanish intelligence (60,000 guerrillas) and French (100,000), their real numerical potential was very scarce. Thus, the supposedly 20,000 Beni Urriaguel warriors would have implied the mobilisation of 30 percent of the whole population, something not achieved even in modern states during the world wars. There are better clues about more realistic data, though. For example, the same Beni Urriaguel warriors who fought against Spain later, went on to form a friendly Harka which had 1,500 warriors and was renewed twice due to the high number of casualties. Therefore, the warlike potential of Beni Urriaguel, the most powerful of all the kabyles, was unlikely more than 3,000-4,500 – or about 7% of the population. This percentage may seem a low figure, but it doubles the percentage of soldiers in arms in the draconian Prussia of Frederick the Great (160,000 out of 4.5 million in 1763) or with the revolutionary fervour of France with the mass levy of 1793 (800,000 from 26 million inhabitants). On the other hand, 7% represents 14% of males, and perhaps 28% of adults. In the end, someone would have to look after the herds, farms and families while the others went to war. Seven percent

would imply slightly less than one in every three fighting-age males going to the front, still exceptional in any case. Other indications of a smaller number of warriors are the other Spanish-friendly Harkas of barely around 100–200 warriors, or at most 1,000. For example, the pro-French Beni Zerual counted 600 warriors in 1925. Another acceptable way of calculating the number of fighters is the number of rifles handed over when the kabyles surrendered. Sanjurjo provided an interesting figure (in SHM, p.171) for 10 July 1927, when 42,000 rifles, 130 cannon, 236 machine guns, eight mortars and five heavy machine guns were requisitioned by Spain. It remains unknown if this figure was for the whole war or only for the final operations, from 1925 onwards. Gárate Córdoba (No. 9, p.286), states that the weapons collected from the enemy in 1929 included 23,103 repeating rifles; 43,112 single shot rifles; 6,175 revolvers; 141 cannons, 30 mortars, 219 complete machine guns, 45 incomplete machine guns, 247 heavy machine guns and 5 incomplete heavy machine guns, and 1,090 aviation bombs. In any case, these amounts could refer to the total number of warriors mobilised by the Rifians, between 1909 and 1927, but not at any one given time. What is certain is that that 14,500 rifles were delivered after the final Spanish offensive in the central Rif, that forced the surrender of Abd el-Krim in May 1926. Therefore, there would have been a similar number of warriors in the central Rif. In the whole Spanish Protectorate 28,000 rifles were taken until October, which gives us a clue about their war potential in the whole rebel Northern Morocco, including areas of Gomara, Lucus and Yebala. For his part, Colonel Capaz accepted the surrender of nine or ten tribes of the Gomara in 1926, collecting 3,000 rifles, that is to say, about 300 per kabyle, and in 1925, 2,000 rifles were taken in the Yebala with the surrender of two or three large kabyles such as Anyera, Hauz and part of Wad Ras. Sumata, on surrendering, gave up 1,000 rifles. Villalobos (p.141), based on French and Spanish intelligence, speaks of 60,000 warriors, although tacitly acknowledging the inflated nature of these numbers, as he qualifies that only 20,000 of them would be armed. Courcelle & Marmié (p.143), speak of 75,000 Rifians under Abd el-Krim in 1924–1925.

12 Federico Villalobos, pp.140–142, mentions 3,000 regulars. Goded, exaggerating, mentions 8,000. Madariaga, p.34, *Desperta Ferro* magazine no. 11, speaks more reasonably of 1,500, and explains in more detail their organisation and functions.

13 Carlos Nogueira Vázquez, *Desperta Ferro* magazine no. 11, pp.25–26.

Chapter 2

1 Federico Villalobos, p.157.

2 Federico Villalobos, pp.155–157. Emilio Marín Ferrer, pp.64–65.

3 Federico Villalobos, pp.157–159.

4 Federico Villalobos, pp.159–162. Emilio Marín Ferrer, pp.65–68, mentions 252 casualties.

5 Federico Villalobos, pp.162–165, reports that some authors affirm that the real casualties were greater, about 1,000. Emilio Marín Ferrer, pp.68–71, speaks of 752 casualties.

6 Perhaps the 1st Inmemorial Del Rey (1st Immemorial of the King) is the oldest regiment in the world, as according to some sources it traces its origins to the Battle of Salado in 1340. Officially, it was created in 1640, and there are other Spanish regiments that come also from the famous Tercios that have their origins before, in the first half of the sixteenth century.

7 Federico Villalobos, pp.165–166 and 168. Sánchez & Kindelán, p.70 for the balloons.

8 Federico Villalobos, pp.167–168.

9 As an aside, the troops that acted in this operation wore for the first time the Wolseley model salacot, of British origin, while the troops of the 1st Division, to the south, were the only ones that continued wearing the Ros kepis, covered with white canvas.

10 Federico Villalobos, pp.168–171, for an overview of the battle. He speaks of 18 casualties in Cavalcanti's forces. For the first part of the battle, up to the cavalry charges, Marín Ferrer is more precise, as well as for Noval's action (pp.76–81 and 84–85).

11 Federico Villalobos, pp.171–173. Emilio Marín Ferrer, pp.81–82, places Aizpuru on the left, Axó in the centre and Primo de Rivera on the right. Villalobos says that only Gorro Frigio remained, and Marín Ferrer that it was Ait Aixa. Villalobos is very critical of this limited

occupation of the Gourougou, but the truth is that Ait Aixa was the key to the whole mountain.

12 Federico Villalobos, pp.173–176. Emilio Marín Ferrer, pp.82–83, mentions 279 casualties.

13 Federico Villalobos, pp.176–177, 289 and 115.

Chapter 3

1 Federico Villalobos, p.179. Emilio Marín Ferrer, p.87. José María Gárate Córdoba, no. 7, p.201.

2 Federico Villalobos, pp.179–180. Emilio Marín Ferrer, pp.88 and 90. José María Gárate Córdoba, no. 7, pp.201–202.

3 Federico Villalobos, pp.179–181 and pp.291–292. According to Emilio Marín Ferrer, pp.88–89, Larrea's column numbered 5,000 soldiers. As for the reinforcements, he cites among others a brigade from Malaga (perhaps he means Villalón's, as he states on p.96), the Half Brigade of the Campo de Gibraltar, and the machine guns of the 1st Brigade of the 3rd Division. These are undoubtedly the same units but citing their geographical origin rather than their official name. He then states that these units formed Ros Souza's 1st Brigade, Carrasco Navarro's 2nd Brigade and Orozco's 3rd Brigade, disagreeing with Villalobos, though perhaps he is referring to a later time.

4 Federico Villalobos, pp.181–182, and 292. Emilio Marín Ferrer, pp.89 and 91. The fighting on 12 September, is detailed in José María Gárate Córdoba, no. 7, pp.211–224.

5 Federico Villalobos, pp.182–184 and 292. According to Emilio Marín Ferrer, pp.91–93, the forces on 15 September were the Melilla Division (with the Ros, Carrasco and Orozco brigades) but Villalón's Expeditionary Forces were only one brigade and the Alcántara Regiment. At the crossing of the Kert, they suffered 69 casualties according to this author.

6 Federico Villalobos, pp.184–185, 118 and 292. Emilio Marín Ferrer, pp.93–94.

7 Federico Villalobos, pp.185–186. Emilio Marín Ferrer, pp.95–96 for the deployment of the columns, cites 292 casualties.

8 Federico Villalobos, pp.186–187. Emilio Marín Ferrer, p.96 for the Malaga Brigade and cavalry units.

9 Federico Villalobos, pp.187–188, refers to only 33 casualties. Emilio Marín Ferrer, pp.96–97. José María Gárate Córdoba, no. 9, pp.265–271, for details of these battles and the composition of the Navarro column and the movements of the northern columns; and Gárate Córdoba, Special issue, for Franco's appearance.

10 Federico Villalobos, pp.188–189. Emilio Marín Ferrer, pp.97–99 speaks of only 5,000 Spaniards in the columns that converged against El Mizzián, but it is probable that he refers only to the closest ones, because the figure of 14,000 Spaniards is García Aldave's own figure. He puts the casualties for the whole campaign at 2,000: 498 dead and 1,587 wounded. José María Gárate Córdoba, no. 9, pp.272–282, for details of the massive offensive of García Aldave, the death of Mizzián and Samaniego, and the withdrawal; Gárate Córdoba Special issue, for Franco.

Chapter 4

1 Federico Villalobos, pp.191–192. On El Raisuni, pp.97–101.

2 Federico Villalobos, pp.192–193. Emilio Marín Ferrer, pp.99–102, for the *Panther* Incident and Silvestre's forces.

3 Federico Villalobos, pp.194–195, and 102 for the words of El Raisuni. Queipo de Llano was the Carabineros commander who in July 1936, alone in a daring action would stand up in Seville and revolt the entire Second Organic Division against the government of the Republic. Then he commanded the Army of the South throughout the war. He would be remembered for his eloquence (his radio serials full of lies and exaggeration to boost the morale of the Nationalists were anthological) as well as for the harshness of the repression in Andalusia.

4 Federico Villalobos, pp.195–196. Emilio Marín Ferrer, pp.103–106, states that there were 30 casualties at the Biutz. Gárate Córdoba, no. 14, pp.419 and 421 for the troops of the Spanish deployment in Ceuta-Tetouan. This deployment had been completed for Larache by the author, based on the *Anuario Militar* of 1914–1916. The *Anuario Militar* is rather tricky, because the location of the units is recorded based on their official HQs for payroll, but not if such

units had been moved to other places for being expeditionary units. Hence, in most records there are only four line regiments and two cavalry regiments in Africa, the only ones officially based there, despite there being some 15 to 20 more regiments deployed there during several years. Also, some regiments had their temporary HQs moved to Africa, so they are recorded in some sections, but not in others of the same Anuario, that still simply records the fixed regiments. There is only one complete register about the location of the regiments in Africa, whether being expeditionary forces, temporary based or fixed based, that is the *Anuario Militar* of 1915. Gárate Córdoba Special issue, for Franco.

5   Sánchez Méndez and Kindelán Camp, pp.72–73. Jaime Velarde Silió, *Aviones Españoles del Siglo XX* (Fundación Infante de Orleans, 2008), pp.42–43. For the Morane, see Cecilio Yusta Viñas, 'La Aviación Militar Española, Nacimiento y Desarrollo Inicial', *Aeroplano Especial*, 29 (Madrid: IHCA, 2011), pp.40–41 and Velarde Silió, pp.38–39.

6   Sánchez Méndez and Kindelán Camp, pp.74–76.

7   Emilio Marín Ferrer, pp.106–107. For details of the formation of the indigenous units, Antonio Carrasco García and de Mesa Gutiérrez, pp.53, 72, 82–83, and 89. Also in Gárate Córdoba, no. 14, pp.423–424.

8   Federico Villalobos, pp.196–197. José María Gárate Córdoba, no. 14, pp.425, 428–435, for the Beni Salem action and pp.445–446 for those of Silvestre and the firefights until April; Gárate Córdoba, no. 15, pp.450–471, for the division/brigades created in the western zone, and the firefights between April and August. Gárate Córdoba, Special issue, for Franco.

9   Sánchez Méndez and Kindelán Camp, pp.76–77 and 79.

10 Sánchez Méndez and Kindelán Camp, pp.76 and 84. Jaime Velarde Silió, pp.44, 46, 49, 55–56 and 61. According to Velarde Silió the date of the crossing over the Gibraltar Strait was on 13 November. Also, at the end of 1919 four DH-9 trainer aircraft were built by Hipano Suiza, but they remained in Cuatro Vientos, Madrid. These examples were used as a model to manufacture them later in Guadalajara (Velarde Silió, p.62).

11 Federico Villalobos, pp.196–197. Emilio Marín Ferrer, pp.107–108.

12 Federico Villalobos, pp.198–200. Emilio Marín Ferrer, pp.109–113, fixes the agreement in a meeting held on 20 May 1916, but it seems that the agreement must have been made in September 1915, as Villalobos states, although Gómez Jordana visited El Raisuni personally afterwards. There, the general found that El Raisuni had 2,000 armed warriors, a figure indicative of the real power of the kabyle, rather more limited and far from Madrid's estimates. The action of the Biutz, in Marín Ferrer. Gárate Córdoba, Special issue, for Franco.

13 Federico Villalobos, pp.200–201. Emilio Marín Ferrer, pp.114–115.

14 Federico Villalobos, pp.201–202. Emilio Marín Ferrer, pp.115–118. This author calls the battery Miscre-la, instead of Mingrela. The first name seems to designate a geographical point, and the second seems to be a Spanish surname. Villalobos affirms that the Moors threw hand grenades, and he mentions that the two reinforcement columns came from Sel-lal and Alcacerseguir, but not those of Barrio and Barrera, cited by Marín Ferrer. They could be the same columns.

15 Federico Villalobos, pp.202–204. Sanjurjo would be the general who between 1922 and 1927 would win the war for Spain, he was also a friend of dictator Primo de Rivera and his military advisor, trusted enough to hold off other commanders, like Franco. Probably he was the most capable commander of the army at an operational level. Later, he would attempt a *coup d'état* in 1932, and then he would be the leader of the 1936 rebellion that ended in the Spanish Civil War, until his death in a strange plane crash left the way open for Franco. Emilio Marín Ferrer, pp.119–120.

16 Federico Villalobos, pp.204–205. Emilio Marín Ferrer, pp.120–123. Vicente Fernández Riera, *Xauen 1924* (Madrid: Almena, 2013), pp.5–6.

17 Federico Villalobos, pp.205–206. Vicente Fernández Riera, pp.10, and 14–15.

18 Federico Villalobos, pp.206–207.

Chapter 5

1   Federico Villalobos, pp.197–198.

2   Antonio Carrasco García and de Mesa Gutiérrez, pp.53, 72, 82–83, and 89.

3   Federico Villalobos, pp.209–210.

4   Federico Villalobos, pp.210–211. Order of battle and movements of the columns according to Carlos de la Rocha's map, Desperta Ferro no. 30, pp.14–15. Colonel Riquelme would be one of the few Africanists who would fight on the Republican side, where he was not very successful as he commanded a conglomerate of militias that were dispersed by the Army of Africa in the advance to Madrid. Emilio Marín Ferrer, pp.125–126.

5   Federico Villalobos, pp.211–214. For Abd el-Krim, pp.117–120. Order of battle and movements of the columns according to Carlos de la Rocha's map, Desperta Ferro no. 30, pp.14–15.

6   Federico Villalobos, pp.215–218. Order of battle of the Villar Column according to Carlos de la Rocha's map, Desperta Ferro no. 30, p.17.

7   Federico Villalobos, pp.217–219. On pages 295 to 296 he includes a breakdown of the troops of the whole Comandancia and their numbers on the payroll, but without removing those who were sick and on leave, as well as those concentrated in Annual. For once, the Spanish estimates of Rifian troops, which were moderate, seemed close to reality. For the Spanish deployment, Carlos de La Rocha's map, Desperta Ferro no. 30, pp.22–23. Calculations of the number of troops made by the author, at the rate of about 150 men per company, Mía, squadron or battery, adding 100 per position for services and per barracks of battalion or regiment. Total number of officers in Marín Ferrer, p.126, who speaks of 100 positions, and not the 48 identified by the author, probably only the larger ones. Circumscriptions and regiments assigned on p.133.

8   Federico Villalobos, pp.219–223. De la Rocha, Desperta Ferro no. 30, p.35, says instead that the column of 17 June was formed by a vanguard under Commander Moreno, of a Tabor and two squadrons, a bulk under Lieutenant Colonel Marina, with three África and three Ceriñola companies (one of machine guns) and a battery, and a rearguard of two Mías. The discrepancy comes from the fact that the África units were probably the relief of the position, so they did not get to fight. Details of the last relief attempt in Marín Ferrer, pp.137–141.

9   Federico Villalobos, pp.224–225. For Emilio Marín Ferrer, p.143, there were three parallel Rifian columns of 2,000 each.

10 Federico Villalobos, pp.224–226. Julio Albi de la Cuesta, 'Preludio de Alhucemas', *Desperta Ferro Contemporánea*, 11 (Madrid: Desperta Ferro, 2015), *Desperta Ferro* magazine no. 30, pp.31–36, mentions that Colonels Marina and Maella shared Silvestre's bewilderment and end in Annual. The version of Silvestre's death in his car mentioned by Villalobos as possible among other versions, is false, since it is known that Silvestre sent his son Ensign Miguel in his car out of the camp (Marín Ferrer, p.143) and Navarro found Silvestre's car with his son beyond Dar Drius on the 22nd. Also absurd is the version that he was condemned in a Council of War improvised by his comrades and forced to commit suicide, which seems a kind of poetic condemnatory sentence for Silvestre's attitude. Marín Ferrer for Silvestre's madness.

11 Emilio Marín Ferrer, pp.143–148. Federico Villalobos, pp.226–227.

12 Emilio Marín Ferrer, pp.148–150 for details of the *Alcántara*. Federico Villalobos, pp.226–227. Miguel Francisco, *Desperta Ferro* magazine no. 30, p.43.

13 Federico Villalobos, pp.226–227. For details of the *Alcántara*'s charges and casualties, Emilio Marín Ferrer, pp 151–155, and Miguel Francisco, *Desperta Ferro* magazine no. 30, pp.38–39 and 43.

14 Emilio Marín Ferrer, pp.167–182. Federico Villalobos, p.228.

15 Federico Villalobos, pp.227–228. Emilio Marín Ferrer, pp.169–188, for the defence of Nador, Selouane and Monte Arruit. De la Rocha, *Desperta Ferro* magazine no. 30, mentions in his map, pp.22–23, a Peninsular Company and four Tabores de Regulares on 15 July in Nador. The Regulares units must have defected before the action, or perhaps they were sent to other sectors of the front. In Selouane instead he only mentions one Tabor de Regulares, so the rest of the

units must have come from other sectors, probably being one of the *Alcántara* squadrons.

16   Emilio Marín Ferrer, pp.157–162.

17   Emilio Marín Ferrer, pp.163–165. De La Rocha, *Desperta Ferro* magazine no. 30, pp.22–23, for the companies of the area.

18   Emilio Marín Ferrer, pp.165–166. De La Rocha, *Desperta Ferro* magazine no. 30, pp.22–23, for the companies of the area.

19   Sánchez Méndez and Kindelán Camp, pp.76 and 84. Jaime Velarde Silió, pp.44, 46, 49, 58 and 61.

20   Sánchez Méndez and Kindelán Camp, pp.85–88 and 78. Jaime Velarde Silió, pp.58 and 61. Probably the DH-4s were purchased but the DH-9s manufactured by the Hispano Suiza.

21   Federico Villalobos, pp.228–229. Miguel Francisco, *Desperta Ferro* magazine no. 30, pp.43 and 46. Hart, quoted by Villalobos, speaks of 18,000 casualties, but the figure does not hold up, since the command had 20,139 men according to the Picasso File, and of them 6,776 were in Melilla, so the casualties would be around 13,000. They could even be fewer, as 3,098 soldiers reported missing came back to Melilla after the disaster, but it is true that the vast majority were wounded in varying degrees, so a large part of them must be considered as casualties, also. Bearing in mind that Spain lost 500 prisoners, the number of dead is easier to calculate: if the number of troops in mobile units and garrisons is subtracted from those who returned, 7,875 soldiers are missing, as Poveda states. On the other hand, Palma Moreno compares the July and August lists, and 8,180 men are missing. Marín Ferrer, p.188, and Villalobos, p.296, agree with these estimates, and citing the deputy Indalecio Prieto speaks of 24,332 soldiers in July, and 11,140 at the end of August, which gives 13,192 casualties, including 4,524 natives and 8,668 Europeans. On the other hand, the bulk of the Regulares and Indigenous Police defected rather than being killed or wounded. Thus, of the 1,383 men of the three infantry Tabors and the cavalry, only 260, including the wounded, 20 percent remained after the disaster. With a few exceptions, therefore, some 1,120 may have defected (or were killed) from these particular units, and the same is true of the Indigenous Police. The probable number of casualties, including defectors, would therefore be 13,000.

By corps, according to Prieto, Ceriñola had 1,158 casualties; San Fernando, 1,993; Melilla, 2,063; África came out relatively intact, with only 480; Alcántara, with 581; Mixed Artillery Regiment, with 588; the Artillery Command, 497; the Engineers, 593; Regulares, 1,599; and Indigenous Police, 3,099 (these two last numbers indicate that the bulk of the natives defected).